Femme Nuna
5/26/14

1

BRIDGING THE GAP

BRIDGING THE GAP

BETWEEN CHRISTIANS AND FILIPINO MUSLIMS

A Memoir by Eufemia Tobias Munn

All Scripture quotations are from The Living Bible (Illustrated) copyright © 1971 by Tyndale House Publishers, Wheaton, Illinois.

Photos courtesy of Buteau's Photography: Blair Elementary School Life Style Photography: Author's photo on book cover

Also by Eufemia Tobias Munn:
         "Moon River on Qingdao Bay"

Edited and published: "A Quest for Excellence in Christian Higher Education"
         By Merton D. Munn

Cover Design: Christian Tobias

DEDICATION

To the memory of my departed loved ones who paved the
way for me to make a difference;

To my family living and serving on four continents;

To all teachers, staff, administrators and Board members of
Shalom Science Institute, who continue to build the bridge
of understanding, peace, and harmony;

To God be the Glory!

ACKNOWLEDGMENT

I am grateful for the encouragement of friends – Dr. Andrew Tsoi, Myrna Pena-Reyes Sweet, Virgilio Gonzales, Dr. Eusebio Kho, Atty. Samuel Buot, and Joseph and Herma Rivera, and especially to my nephew, Christian Tobias, who had ignited the spark for me to write, read the final manuscript and publish on Amazon Kindle.

My special appreciation goes to Doug Griffith, who patiently organized and edited the manuscript; to my literary agent, Corazon Pasaporte Horder, I owe a great deal of gratitude.

TABLE OF CONTENTS

Page

Foreword

FOREWORD

My life is a story. "Bridging the Gap" chronicles my journey from World War II – I survived the Japanese, the Muslim raiders, malaria, and leeches in the jungle – to building a bridge of understanding, peace, and harmony through education across religious and cultural barriers in my hometown, Balabagan, Lanao del Sur, Philippines

I am a descendant of immigrants in the 1920's from Cebu in the Central Visayas, who acquired tracts of land as "homesteads" in Lanao del Sur, a province with a large Muslim population.

Walk with me in my journey as the woven tapestry of events unravel through education at Silliman University in the Philippines and Whitworth University in Spokane, Washington; marriage to Dr. Merton Munn, Presbyterian missionary to Silliman University, my service at Silliman, the United Board for Christian Higher Education in Asia in New York, at Lakeland Village in Medical Lake, Washington, and Sheldon Jackson College in Sitka, Alaska, and as Principal of Blair Elementary School on Fairchild Air Force Base in Spokane, Washington.

I survived the turmoil and challenges after my husband's death. Meandering through widowhood in search for a life with purpose, I decided to help build and develop Shalom Science Institute, a non-profit Christian school in Balabagan. It was a turning point in my retirement, one that has taken me to China to teach for four years and to Chile for two years to generate funds to build the school.

From experiencing with leeches in the jungle in the Philippines, to viewing the vast expanse of China from the Great Wall, and to climbing the Moia Statue quarry in Easter Island in

2007 is a span of sixty-six years! I continue bridging the gap between Christians and Filipino Muslims in Balabagan, my hometown. My story is far from over!

CHAPTER 1

"When you go through deep waters and great trouble, I will be with you.
When you go through rivers of difficulty, you will not drown!
When you go through the fire of oppression, you will not be burned up.
The flames will not consume you." (Isaiah 43:2 TLB)

ESCAPE TO THE JUNGLE

Bombs rocked the Island of Oahu in Hawaii; billows of smoke engulfed the United States Naval Base in Pearl Harbor on December 7, 1941. The attack by the Japanese triggered the spread of World War II to the Pacific; its ripples reached the shores of the Philippine Islands in a short time. That "day of infamy" changed my life forever.

Schools closed and education came to an abrupt end. My oldest sister, Jovencia, who was in teacher-training in Bukidnon Normal School in Malaybalay, as well as my parents' friends -- the Hofer brothers, Arturo, Andres, and Vicente at Silliman University in Dumaguete City, Negros Oriental had to come home. My older brothers Virgilio, Constancio, and Jeremias came home from Malabang public schools, eleven kilometers away. My parents – Cayetano "Papa" a very social and hardworking man, and Gabriela "Mama" always quiet and supportive, were sad that schooling was disrupted, but grateful that all their children were home. At that time, Mama had a 10-month old baby, Rachel. There were nine of us ranging in age from 10 months to 17 years. I was the seventh child, and I had just turned 4 years old two weeks before Pearl Harbor was bombed.

There was a great commotion that day in our yard, where Papa had rice and corn mills and an abaca stripper—strips fiber from abaca stalks. Our home was along the national highway and it was a hub of homesteaders, who brought their produce to be processed. They came with loaded "karomata" – a wooden cart pulled by carabao, a "beast of burden" used in plowing fields and pulling carts. Milling had stopped and people talked in loud voices, and I could hear, "Japanese! Japanese!" I watched this scene from my favorite perch on a walk-up breezeway, which divided our kitchen from the main house.

It did not take long before the Japanese invaded the Philippines. There was news of advancing troops, and sounds of airplanes sent us running for cover in bushes or under trees. We and many other families escaped to the jungle, a few kilometers hike from the highway.

Life in the jungle was fraught with hardship. Food had to be brought in surreptitiously in the night under cover of darkness. Cooking had to be done at night because during the day smoke would have given us away to the enemy. We lived in a one-room makeshift shelter made of   thatched roof, bamboo slats for floor, woven coconut fronds (palapad) for walls and water had to be carried in bamboo tubes on shoulders from a small stream. I had taken baths with water scooped with tiny pail from the stream. Sunshine filtered through a thick canopy of trees creating a beautiful sight and we were safe from low flying airplanes. But underneath was a thick carpet of dead, damp leaves – the perfect habitat of leeches! These slimy bloodsuckers quickly became my greatest enemies! I walked barefoot, and they attached themselves to my legs and could not be pulled off until they had their fill of my blood. I would run to the stream, but had to walk back with a bamboo tube of water on my shoulder – trying in vain to avoid all the leeches.

We used the jungle refuge for nearly a year but intermittently came home when it was fairly safe. During one of those times, Jovencia – always calm, steady and the tallest of my sisters -- and Andres Hofer (a "mestizo") whose father came from Switzerland, announced their engagement in his parents' home in Banago. It was late afternoon when they came home and found me in the breezeway. Jovencia told me that they were getting married soon.

I savored the excitement of the wedding celebration and watched the preparations from the breezeway. Men dripping in sweat had been roasting pigs skewered in bamboo poles over hot coals. (The preparation of a large feast for a social gathering in Filipino culture is as interesting as the event itself.) People in the cooking area seemed to be having a good time –chopping, cooking, and talking. They grabbed this chance to be oblivious of the War and to enjoy a happy occasion. I saw the tents being set up for eating and dancing. It was a wonderful wedding and afterwards, Jovencia and Andres would join his family in Banago.

In addition to the Japanese, we worried about Muslim raiders, too. There had been an escalation of Muslim raids on some homes in remote areas. In the weeks after Jovencia and Andres' wedding, Papa and others were on high alert. Fearful of Muslim raiders, two families evacuated to our home. The adults were welcome because they could help Papa and Mama make plans for evacuation. Food had never been a problem because we had a large room for rice, root crops, bunches of bananas, corn, pineapple, and dried beans. There was always a good supply of avocado, jackfruit, and papaya on our property. Chickens and pigs were around to butcher for food.

Our home had been built for a large family. The kitchen had a long dining table with wooden benches made by Papa from lumber hewn from trees on the farm.   The main house had three bedrooms on one side and my parents' bedroom on the opposite side. The center was a huge open space with wooden benches along the walls. The hardwood floor was polished by using half coconut husks. The person polishing would stand on one foot and use the other foot to vigorously move the husk back and forth. The floor was nice; people just sat down on it.

At the start of the War it was the place for singing during anxious evenings. The families who had joined us had children and young adults. One song I remember is "Sentimental Journey." Nobody cared to explain to me what it meant. I was just a four-year old who sat alone on the floor in a corner of the large living room, but it remains in my memory of that time.

Our house had an attic with a secret passage, but to my consternation I had been forbidden to climb the secret ladder. Oh, but I did, one afternoon when no one was around. Up there I saw piles of boxes and bundles. Papa and my brothers had put away things that we couldn't carry in case we had to evacuate. I descended shaken, not from Papa's possible scolding, but from reality that we might have to leave this home. Later, I learned that Papa had another secret place. It was a huge hollow trunk of a fallen tree where he stored valuables like a sewing machine and china. I actually went there with him once. It was dark inside but he had a flashlight. The thought of snakes had prevented me from going in with him. I had been afraid of snakes since Papa had shot one slithering on a tree at twilight. It had tried to kill a chicken asleep on a branch.

TERROR AT DUSK

Then, it happened, just as dusk had given way to complete darkness. Muslim raiders armed with guns and machetes invaded our home! They came upstairs and ordered all of us to go down to the yard at gunpoint. We were encircled and guarded, while others looted everything they found including a pot of rice for our dinner. Loaded, they finally left us shuddering in the evening heat. We could have all been killed that very hour! I had been terrified looking at men with guns, with the memory of what happened to that snake still lingering in my mind. Papa spoke to one he had recognized, who told him that in such a time as this, he was no longer a friend.

Light had just started to break in the eastern skies when we left. We would walk eleven kilometers from our homestead home in barrio Itil to Banago on the coast to join Jovencia and Andres. As skinny as a rail, all I could carry was a winnower – a flat woven basket. Adults carried bundles and baskets on shoulders and heads. Mama carried Baby Rachel, tied to her waist, while toddler Josue was on my brother Constancio's shoulder. My older sisters Remy and Josephine carried bamboo tubes with drinking water on their shoulders. It was a cloudless sunny day and by noon, the scorching heat made the trek on a rugged and narrow trail more difficult.

I became tired, hungry, and began crying. The heat of noonday sun baked my tear-drenched face. We had stopped to rest and eat. From the front of the line, I stretched my neck out to look back at all the adults and children. I peeled my banana carefully so not a morsel of it would fall. With that and rationed swallows of water from a bamboo tube, I regained my strength. We were midway to our destination, but the last half took the most out of me. Tatay, my grandfather, tall, handsome and part Spanish with a long distinguished nose, had offered to carry me on his back. He was already loaded with live chickens in a basket (bukag). No more tears. I just had to force my feet to move one in front of the other. We reached Banago without any Japanese airplanes or Muslim raiders. Most of the way had been in the open – cogon grass and coconut trees - with no place to hide. God was with us! Jovencia and Andres were there, waiting for us.

When we reached the beach, the pale sunset and gentle lapping of the waves lulled me   to sleep. I was awakened by Mama's call for supper. Papa said grace. Supper consisted of rice, boiled shellfish and fish, broiled on a pile of coconut shell coals. I looked at the large eyes of a broiled big green fish on banana leaves. What a welcome sight! "Where are we?"I asked.

Moonrise caught us still eating. In the midst of fear, the question had been asked, "Where next?" We had run away from Muslim raiders who had infiltrated Christian homesteads. (Later, we were told that after we left our home, the raiders had returned and had taken all of Papa's machinery and equipment for his corn and rice mills, and his abaca stripper and the house was burned.) We knew that the Japanese garrison was in Cotabato City, a few hours away by land. We had left our home in haste and in fear of Muslim raiders and Japanese soldiers, but also to me, I had left my greatest enemy - leeches in the jungle.

SAFETY IN SULTANATE PROTECTION

In the midst of chaos and fear was rising compassion and hope. Our parents' unwavering faith transcended the chaos and fear in our young minds and nurtured us in the manner in which hope prevails in times of peace and war.

Huddled in Banago for what had seemed a very long time, though it must only have been a few weeks, an invitation came from Sultan Sampiano of Barorao, a neighboring barrio, to come to his sultanate. (A territory or an area ruled and protected by a sultan or a sovereign.) He was a very kind-hearted and compassionate Muslim; there was gentleness in him that made Christians feel welcome and safe. We moved to his sultanate to be under his protection.

In Barorao, my family began making soap out of lye and coconut oil. The soap formula is still a mystery to me, but to a five year old there were mountains of soap bars. My job was to count them. It was a good business, but procuring supplies became a problem. Outside the bounds of the sultanate, safety was precarious at best. My baby brother Abraham and nephew, James had been born in Barorao. There were rumors of Japanese troops approaching Barorao, just a few hours by land from Cotabato. We had to evacuate! Where?

LIFE IN RICE PADDIES

My parents had heard of Bobong, Cotabato, where rice grew in abundance and within the protection of the Sinsuat and Pendatun families. Datu Blo Sinsuat and General Salipada Pendatun, like Sultan Sampiano, provided protection to Christians.

16

Under cover of darkness, our family, including Jovencia and Andres, left Bororao, huddled inside a banca - a wooden boat with bamboo outriggers. We joined a few boats to paddle downriver to the sea. I found myself crouched at the bottom of the banca close to my baby brother, Abraham. It was daylight when we arrived in Bobong, welcomed by a vast expanse of golden rice fields ready for harvest. Our family claimed a corner in a large rice warehouse filled with evacuees. In Bobong, my brothers harvested rice and caught fresh water fish "katipa" and "haloan" in rice paddies.

We eventually moved out of the big building into a house. Our family used the downstairs for a small business – clothes repair, sewing and coffee shop. I still remember vividly that Papa had to rip and unwind fine cotton foot socks carefully so that Mama could use the thread in sewing. Jovencia managed the coffee shop; we served fried camote (sweet potato), and fried bananas. My job was to count Japanese paper money at night by a coconut oil lamp. I did this upstairs while taking care of Baby James. His father, Andres, had to stay away or work behind closed doors because he was wanted by the Japanese. Our family worked hard for a good supply of rice and fish, business was fine, but Bobong was near Cotabato City with the headquarters of Japanese military and garrisons.

TAPIAN – LAST EVACUATION PLACE

Once again, our group had to evacuate. Our "armada" of evacuees had to paddle furiously to Tapian across the bay from Cotabato City. We joined many families in a huge house on a coconut plantation. In those days, people with white skin and foreign names were on the Japanese "Wanted List." The Spanish owners had to escape to the hills because they were wanted by the Japanese, so evacuees stayed there.

The coconut plantation with a magnificent view of the ocean was a haven. The long stretch of beach became the children's playground and adults fished during the day and night. We had coconuts for making oil and bountiful seafood was for the taking. However, rice had to be procured from Bobong by bartering with oil and dried fish. Sometimes, people had to risk their lives to find rice.

Once, on their way to Bobong in a small banca, Andres and his nephew were captured by the Japanese and were taken prisoners because their last name was Hofer. They were on the "Wanted List!" On that trip with them were Jovencia and her little son, James. Fortunately, the Japanese soldiers took them back to shore. We had to help her go through the ordeal of her husband being held prisoner and fearing for his life.

We had moved into our own house on the plantation and my chores included mending clothes and helping Mama and Jovencia make Japanese flags to wave to Japanese soldiers when they came. I could not remember what material we used for flags, but I had to make red circles. I also took my sickly little sister, Rachel, for walks.

On our favorite trail to the mangroves, there was a narrow foot bridge over a pool of water that rose and ebbed with the tide. I had noticed that fish would jump onto the rocks and would take time to get back in water. I had decided to catch them with bare hands and throw them near Rachel on higher ground. I caught a lot of fish, tied them with coconut leaves and carried them home. The load was heavy but we were happy. Soon I

18

realized that Rachel was walking on her own with a string of fish. The excitement had helped her get better. We made our daily walk to that spot, but there were no more fish to catch. The people had used nets and depleted our source of fish.

I loved Tapian! My younger brother Josue and I made tide pools and coral reefs our   playground at low tide. We would go out with Tatay, when he would set his fish traps and harvest fish during the next low tide. We caught crabs in mangroves and also in water lilies at high tide. We would swim to those lilies and catch crabs embedded in them. Little Rachel would watch us, as well as our basket of crabs.

For a time in Tapian, we enjoyed the luxury of space, a long stretch of beach, coral reefs and tide pools, but soon a Japanese encampment was established closer to us. Sometimes we had to escape to the hills. There, life was hard. Again, we had to trek hillsides and carry water in bamboo tubes, and food was scarce. We subsisted on dried fish and rice cooked with sweet potato. We raised ducks and chickens and planted a vegetable garden but the hillside was dry. My daily chore was to take a family of ducks to a tiny stream with shallow pools of water for them to swim. One day, it was dark by the time I gathered them all to walk back to the house. I discovered a little duckling was missing, and I worried what had happened to it in the night.

When news came that the Japanese had pulled out of their camp, we returned to Tapian. Soon after our return, Andres collapsed at our doorstep. He had escaped from the Japanese prison. He was emaciated after six months of torture and food deprivation. Tatay and my grandmother, Nanay, short and petite of pure Malayan stock, nursed Andres back to health.   (The shortest among my siblings, I inherited Nanay's height.)

19

Through the War years, Tatay and Nanay had become a "medicine couple" to the whole community of evacuees. They used herbs, roots, bark, fruit and coconut for medicine. Undiluted coconut milk squeezed from freshly grated coconut meat was used for laxative. Boiled ginger root (salabat) was used for nausea, colds, and sore throat. The fruit and leaves of bitter melon (ampalaya) were used for malaria. (I had suffered with chills and convulsions from a severe case of malaria, so I had to eat bitter melon – fruit or leaves until I was well.) They also delivered babies, and assisted parents in caring for their babies. Our youngest brother, Ben, was born in Tapian, and I remember Tatay and Nanay added leaves of "dalapot" (a broad-leaf plant) to the water in the basin to bathe him.

In Tapian we were free from fear of Muslims who took advantage of the War to raid and burn homes of Christians, but the Japanese had become more ferocious. Fortunately for us, we were spared horrible events.

Our faith sustained us through all those years, and we constantly prayed for General Douglas MacArthur's return.

CHAPTER 2

"I will open up rivers for them on high plateaus!
I will give them fountains of water in the valleys!
In the desert will be pools of water, and rivers fed
by springs shall flow across the dry, parched ground."
(Isaiah 41:18 TLB)

"I SHALL RETURN"

General Douglas MacArthur's promise to return to the Philippines to liberate the country from Japanese occupation had helped us survive our terrible experiences of World War II. For four years we had lived in spite of constant fear, scarcity of food and sickness of several kinds. We had had to run away from two enemies – the Japanese and Muslim raiders. We sought refuge in the jungle, hiked to a friendly sultanate for protection and had evacuated to other places in bancas. Then towards the end of the War the Japanese had become more ferocious and committed terrifying acts.

LIBERATION FROM JAPANESE OCCUPATION

A deep and booming sound from the ocean shattered the stillness of the night and awakened us. It was early dawn. As daylight started to break through darkness, out in the ocean we saw huge ships – carriers! Airplanes had started to fly off those carriers and were dropping bombs on Cotabato City! Then the airplanes would come out from billows of smoke and fly back to the carriers in "V" formation. The city was in smoke for days. We saw the massive bombardment of Japanese garrisons from just across the bay!

I was eight years old and had just recovered from malaria when the American forces arrived. The lame and the sick found the strength to walk to the beach to join a throng of people in jubilation and rejoicing! We had waited for this for four years, and now we were witnessing the fulfillment of General Douglas MacArthur's promise - "I shall return."

Then a fleet of amphibian transports headed to our shore from those ships. We were ready to welcome them! The American soldiers came ashore with boxes of food, chocolate and candy. We had coconuts and all kinds of fruits. I had carried a hand (sipi) of ripe banana but adults had gone ahead of me. One soldier saw me and two other children behind the crowd and approached us. Seeing this giant face-to-face was overwhelming! I gave him the banana that I was carrying. I could not say a word. I just cried. He gave us chewing gum and chocolate. It was a very happy day! We were liberated from the Japanese! This most anticipated joyous event totally cured me of malaria and I never had a recurrence of this malady.

In jubilation and thanksgiving, people started plans to return to their homes. My brother, Jeremias took food and went to fetch Tatay and Nanay a kilometer away to join in making plans. Along the way, he was tempted to open two cans of sardines and enjoyed every bit of them. He was so ecstatic!

It was not long before our family was loaded in a banca with a sail to go from Tapian Point in Cotabato province back to Malabang, Lanao del Sur. I don't recall how long the voyage took. I remember our stopover on Bongo Island, about mid-way to our destination. There were several boats with us and Bongo was a perfect respite for the weary war survivors. I waded in tide pools in search of live shellfish to eat. Josue caught an octopus, and

Jeremias found sea urchins and anemones. Mama at this time was not feeling well. She delegated all the cooking to my sisters.

The sea was calm and we finally reached our destination - Malabang, The town was crowded with survivors of the War – Muslims and Christians – who would eventually return to their own areas, just as we would.

In Malabang, our house was near a spring of clear water flowing from sides of boulders. It was perfect for swimming and doing laundry, but we had to carry water to the house. Andres, Virgilio, and Constancio were hired at Malabang airport working with American soldiers. Through them, we had a good supply of food from the USA, including condensed milk which we used for Baby Ben. I prepared his milk bottle - a mix of hot water and condensed milk- and took care of him. Mama by this time was really sick and could not nurse him. Four years of war with young children to take care of and feed had taken a toll on her health. Tatay and Nanay had to work hard to nurse her back to health.

The airport jobs of my brothers helped us tremendously. They had been befriended by Americans who wanted to take them back to the USA, but my parents objected. Andres built a house for him and Jovencia. I remember the kitchen floor was surplus "steel matting" from the airport. I spent a lot of time with them taking care of James. Since their house was in a good location in town, Papa set up a barbershop there. His clients were mostly Americans.

Mama's health soon greatly improved. Five of us children enrolled in Malabang Elementary School. Jeremias, with a pleasant personality, loving, and caring, was in sixth grade and was a good student. As a first grader, I had great admiration for him. He was kind, patient, and a smart student. He helped me with school work, especially arithmetic. One day Virgilio and Constanclo had come home from the airport with surplus parachutes – very fine material. Mama sewed dresses for us three girls in school and shirts for my younger brothers. It had been quite a sight to see us in our "parachute" clothes. I had red, white and blue dresses. I was happy and proud to wear them.

In school we learned to recite the "U.S. Pledge of Allegiance" and to sing "The Star Spangled Banner." At every Monday morning's flag ceremony, both the United States and the Philippine flags would be hoisted on poles and we would sing both anthems and say the pledges of allegiance of both countries.

Then everything changed on July 4. 1946! The Philippines was granted Independence from the United States and we no longer recited the U.S. Pledge of Allegiance nor sang the "Star Spangled Banner." I cried! I had not understood it at all as a first grader. As an eight year-old survivor of World War II, singing the "Star Spangled Banner" was the ultimate redemption from an interrupted education during the War and a reminder that we had been liberated by the Americans. Suddenly, it ended! I was confused and sad.

RETURN TO OUR HOMESTEAD

At the end of my first grade our family returned to our homestead in barrio Itil. Life was hard during the first few months of our return to the homestead but we were happy. A palm leaf (nipa) hut had been built as our temporary shelter while a big house was constructed of hand-hewn lumber and native materials. Trees were felled for fields to plant corn and other crops, and there was an abundance of fruit trees – avocado, jackfruit, oranges, lemons, and a jungle of papaya trees and bananas.

Towards the end of that first summer we had to guard the corn field from hungry, menacing monkeys. Papa built a tree house near the edge of the field. My brother, Josue and I were assigned as guards, armed with firecrackers. I had loved the view from up there. We were able to see troops of monkeys, who would stealthily creep from the jungle. As soon as they had reached the edge of the corn field, we would throw firecrackers at them. They would jump and sprint as fast as lightning back to the jungle, frightened by the loud noise.

Education was very important to my parents. As soon as we moved back to our homestead, they realized that Malabang was too far away for us to attend school, so they asked, "Why not build a school that would serve all children in the area?"

So they donated two hectares of our property to the Public School. (This was my first introduction to philanthropy.) Papa mobilized volunteers to build the classrooms. Most of the materials were supplied by the public school. Three months later, classrooms were ready, and a principal and teachers were hired by the start of school year. **Itil Elementary School** was born! It's location along the national highway was ideal. The new teachers who had been hired stayed with us temporarily until they had found housing.

I entered second grade in that new school. By the end of third grade, I was accelerated to fifth for the following year. (Itil Elementary School still exists. I visited it in 2000 and in 2010. The current Principal serves on the Board of Shalom Science Institute, my project in Balabagan.)

It was most convenient to have a school next to our home. After school and on weekends, I tended a roadside papaya stand when I was not on guard duty for monkeys in the tree house. Buses plying between Cotabato and Malabang often stopped and passengers bought and ate a lot of papaya. I had enjoyed it so much because of the money I earned, but I had to gather papaya myself and carry them in baskets to the stand. That was a hard job! Fortunately, family members often helped me. The sap of papaya fruit made my hands tender.

School and our life on our homestead had been wonderful! It was a big surprise, therefore, when Papa announced that he had sold it and we would move to Davao province.

We had survived the hardships of World War II and had been liberated to return to our homestead to live in peacetime. In the short time since we came home, the farm was flourishing and Itil Elementary School was right at our doorstep – a dream of my parents. Why move to Davao? It was an unanswered question. I was too young to understand and no one shared the decision with me.

CHAPTER 3

"Ask, and you will be given what you ask for. Seek, and you will find.
Knock, and the door will be opened. For everyone who asks, receives.
Anyone who seeks, finds. If only you will knock, the door will open."
(Mathew 7:7-8 TLB)

NO TURNING BACK

The Homestead Act of the Philippine Commonwealth Government in the 1900's encouraged emigration to the big island of Mindanao in the southern Philippines. My paternal grandparents and my maternal grandmother had been in a wave of emigrants from Cebu Island in the Central Visayas. Papa and Mama had met and married in Pikit, Cotabato. Years later, they joined other emigrants and settled in the province of Lanao del Sur, which had a large Muslim population. Several families settled there in the late 1930's and a Christian community of homesteaders evolved. (I was the first child born in the area.) My parents, uncle and grandparents eventually acquired titles to tracts of land that became their homesteads. It had taken my parents a long time to acquire their homestead. Now they sold it lock, stock and barrel. But they left a part of that homestead behind with the two hectares of land donated to Itil Elementary School.

I could not understand why we had to move to another province, one that Papa had not even visited! He was not alone. My grandparents, uncle, Jovencia and Andres also sold their homesteads and moved to Davao province. Many of Papa's friends made the same decision. Years later he told us that his fear of Muslims during the War had become greatly embedded in him that he had to move his family to a province with Christian population. It was a leap of faith for my parents to pack and load their family on a bus and take the long land trip to Davao.

Our family settled in Padada, Davao del Sur - a land of cornfields and coconuts. We occupied a corner of a huge corn warehouse with other families from Lanao del Sur, while our own house was constructed. The warehouse was located in the middle of a very large corn farm, which had been operated as a cotton plantation by the Japanese before World War II. Now the owner allowed us children to glean after the corn harvest, which was done by machines. The field became a playground and gleaning was fun.

Soon we moved into our new two-bedroom house - the same design as that of Papa's close friend who had convinced him to move away from Lanao del Sur province. Papa lined the balcony with potted bougainvilleas. It was beautiful! Jovencia and Andres moved in with us until they could relocate to another area in Davao province. Their second child, Jill, and our youngest sister, Fely, were born in that house. With her birth our family had now grown to six brothers and six sisters, making us a family of fourteen! The two oldest had married. Two years later, our parents extended their welcome to our cousins Arturo and Dominico Moreno to join our family. Their mother was my mother's sister and their parents died during the War.

EDUCATION, CHURCH, AND HOME LIFE

Padada had a primary school only, so my sisters Remy, Josephine and I attended sixth grade in Guihing Elementary School, four kilometers away; all three of us graduated from sixth grade in 1950. A couple across the street from the school had opened their home for children who brought lunch. Sometimes we spent the noon hours in Guihing River swimming and eating our lunch there. We loved the river! On Saturdays, we took the bus with loads of laundry, washed as fast as we could, put everything to dry on sand bars and had fun swimming, while waiting for the laundry to dry.

Our day at home started with morning devotion. Papa had gone to evangelistic meetings in his youth and had already become a Protestant when he married Mama, who was Roman Catholic. In fact, their first four children were baptized both in the Protestant and Roman Catholic churches. The Philippines is predominately Catholic and it was unusual for a family to become Protestants in those days. By the time I came along, it was already a Protestant household, although we spent many times through the years in Catholic prayer meetings with Popo, my maternal grandmother, who lived with my aunt and uncle. I don't recall how old I was when I learned to pray, but I remember Papa's very lengthy prayers, even at mealtimes. When Fely was five years old, she was asked to say grace. We closed our eyes and she said,

"Let us pray. Lord, number one. Amen."

The family burst into laughter at this short but poignant prayer! She explained that she had memorized four prayers and when hungry, she'd say the number one, the shortest. "And the Lord knows what it is," she said.

I understood perfectly what Fely meant. Her words reminded me of what Mama had said once when I asked her if she had understood her Latin prayer. She said, "Not exactly, but God knows what it means."

We had inherited good genes from our parents. They had also taught us Christian core values that they themselves modeled

29

for us. When I had lunch with Rev. Jerry Aninon in Davao City in 1997, he said, "You and your siblings have become what you are because of your parents. They were wonderful Christians." Jerry had lived with us when he was first pastor of Padada United Church of Christ.

On Sundays after church our home became the hub of worshippers from the barrios who had brought lunch. It was always a big Sunday gathering. Papa was a layman but was instrumental in planting new churches. He was a founder of Padada United Church of Christ and later, Malalag United Church of Christ both in Davao del Sur.

My parents' mixed marriage was strong, despite differences in their religion. They desired for us a level of formal education they had not attained. Mama had only a sixth grade education because Popo, her mother, believed that girls only need to learn to sew, cook, garden and embroider. She excelled in all those skills but there was always an insatiable desire in her for more. Papa, an only child, had quit school at seventh grade when my grandparents immigrated to Mindanao. There was no school near where they lived.

My parents had raised us in the best Christian way that they knew. Mama had that gentle quietness in her that I came to admire. She shed silent tears and Papa was the disciplinarian. The rod was not spared and Papa's word was the law of the house. Nobody in my family dared to talk back, until one day, I said, "You are not always right, you know."

Oops! I thought my world would crumble, but Papa had just sat there in silence. At that time, my older sisters, Josephine and Remy, had started to wear lipstick and to go to movies. I had wanted him to think that those were fine, especially for Remy, who had participated in a beauty queen contest. My parents had noticed a pre-teen rebellion in me because I always spoke for my sisters. There was no high school where we lived, but the incident probably precipitated my exile to a Christian school far away from home.

Papa escorted Josephine and me to Midsayap, Cotabato, a long land trip and enrolled us in the high school department of Southern Christian College (SCC). We were first year students. We lived with Aunt Angela, Mama's younger sister, whose house was next to Midsayap United Church of Christ. In order to earn our keep for board and room, we helped our Aunt in her business. She had set up a halo-halo stand across the street from Southern Christian College. (Halo- halo is a mix of fruit, cooked beans, sugar, milk, and ice shaving.) After school, Josephine and I had to pick up blocks of ice packed in sacks and carried them on our heads. The ice plant may not have been very far but to me, it was a long distance to walk with a load on my head! We would shave the ice for halo-halo.

Josephine excelled in sports and became popular. (Her coach, Josue Rodriguez, years later, became my neighbor at Silliman University in Dumaguete City.) Watching Josephine in sports had made me proud of her but I was not interested in sports. I was into my small world of academics with two friends, Nelly, a Seventh Day Adventist, and Lina, a Roman Catholic. Both girls had attended the high school department of Southern Christian College for its quality education. From Mrs. Helen Abrenica, our English teacher, and Mr. Bagua Buat, a Muslim, our excellent math teacher, I learned to love English and mathematics.

Then, "Character Education," a class with the New Testament for the text, expanded what I had learned from my parents and church. I had had Bible lessons in Sunday school, but this was my introduction to formal Bible study. At 12 years old, my mind became a sponge. I listened and absorbed the implications of what Prof. Yasay taught. The lessons I learned strengthened the foundation for my strong faith. When I went home a year later my parents noticed the change in me and were thrilled.

While Josephine and I were away, Southeastern Institute, a non-sectarian private school had been in development in our hometown, Padada. It opened its doors by next school year, so she and I continued our high school there. Our sister, Remy, also enrolled there. Some classes were held in a movie theater with a dirt floor, while classrooms were being constructed. My science and geometry classes were held there. The science teacher was not only excellent, but came impeccably dressed and in high-heeled shoes despite the dirt and mud. That had left a deep impression on me on how a teacher should present herself in class.

I had a good English teacher at Southeastern Institute, but at the end of my sophomore year, she had to return to her home in Argao, Cebu. Her replacement was excellent in drama, and I got hooked! This teacher had me play the role of Mother Superior in "Half an Hour in a Convent," by Luis Ma. Guerrero. Every Friday afternoon for weeks, we had gone to Holy Cross Academy in Digos, Davao, to observe the nuns. I had wanted to surprise my parents, so the night of the performance, Papa, a Protestant, had the biggest surprise of his life to see his daughter in a nun's habit! Mama, a Catholic was elated. Another surprise to my parents was my role as a villain in a community play during a town fiesta. It was directed by the same teacher. I loved to perform! By that time, Papa and Mama were reconciled to my free spirit and were proud of my participation in many school and community activities.

At the end of my senior year, I was awarded the "Golden Cup," a coveted prize for first place in the oratorical contest on "I Speak for Democracy." In a light blue gown, which Mama had made for me, I stood in front of a huge crowd in the public plaza and had delivered my speech. It was a great gift for my parents and family. "I Speak for Democracy" was a very heavy topic for a 16-year old, but I had enjoyed preparing so much, and my enjoyment and success led to more contests in the province.

The first class of high school graduates from Southeastern Institute, only had four graduates – Josephine, me, and two others. There was no ceremony, but the quality of education we had received was outstanding. My senior year in high school ended without fanfare in March 1954.

In retrospect, my parents' decision to move our family to Davao benefited us after all. Right in Padada, our town, we had the opportunity to attain our high school education. I realized then the importance of a school's proximity to children and young people, a conviction that shaped my future.

CHAPTER 4

*"If I ride the morning winds to the farthest oceans,
even there your hand will guide, your strength will support me.
If I try to hide in the darkness, the night becomes light around me."
(Psalm 139:9-11 TLB)*

ON THE WINGS OF WIND

College education was just a dream - a wish - when I finished high school at Southeastern Institute. Sequestered in the quiet town of Padada about a hundred kilometers from Davao City, I had been resigned to the idea that going to college was far in the future. However, I was determined to make the best of any circumstance I was in. My sister, Josephine had been recruited to attend Brokenshire School of Nursing. She would have been one of the first students. However, my parents objected that it was too far away, but the real reason was the major expense of a boarding house and upkeep. What they envisioned was a "home" in the city where both she and I could attend college. That was not possible. At the time, I had only heard a vague mention of Silliman University at the start of World War II when Andres Hofer had to come home.

My parents decided to start a new farm in Caputian, Malalag. Josephine and I stayed in Padada; she worked in a dress shop. I was the housemother to Abraham and Ben, who were in grade school and to our youngest sister – four-year old Fely. I remember we had to do laundry when it rained because the artesian well water was very hard. Abraham skipped school and sometimes I would find him hiding behind various trees and bushes. He told me that he did not like his teacher, so I had long conferences with his teacher. Ben had been doing well in school and Fely was a delightful girl. I made her a dress by hand-sewing – fine checkered cotton with ruffles on the shoulders – my first venture at sewing. I had her help me with everything I did, including the work in our large vegetable garden. She was able to help me wrap every single "ampalaya" (bitter melon) fruit with newspaper. Our parents came home some weekends and Sundays were special because of our active participation in church. We would only occasionally spend our weekends at the farm. Looking back, I was a good housemother for the children.

Then Jovencia visited. She and Andres had returned to Lanao del Sur and had relocated in Balabagan, eleven kilometers from Itil. She asked Papa and Mama to let me assist in the grocery business that she had established in Balabagan. They agreed, so I went with her to help in the business. Located near the beach, I readily settled in. I missed the children, but by that time they could live on the farm with our parents so the boys transferred to a nearby school. I missed the Padada United Church of Christ in the Philippines (UCCP). There was no UCCP church in Balabagan at that time. Still, I decided early on in my youth that I would do the best wherever I was and would leave the rest to God.

Balabagan Coconut Estate (BCE), which comprised a thousand hectares of coconut trees, had gone into massive development to grow abaca (hemp for ropes) and cassava (food root crop). It operated a thriving cassava flour mill. All kinds of jobs brought in engineers; accountants; agriculturists; field managers; experts with machinery and farm equipment; cassava mill technicians and a labor force. Andres was a field manager for abaca farm development. The BCE had an airstrip, a Catholic Church, its own electric generators and even movie house. A public school was within walking distance. Since a natural spring runs through the main hub of the property and there was a beach nearby, it was an ideal place for employees and families to socialize. Employment at BCE fueled the economy of Balabagan.

Jovencia had a close relationship with Mrs. Maria Clara Lobregat, owner of Balabagan Coconut Estate. She was kind and gracious. (A few years later, she left BCE and became active in politics: she was a delegate to the Constitutional Convention, served as a Congresswoman and later, became Mayor of Zamboanga City.)

Andres and Jovencia's home was a kilometer outside BCE. When I joined their household, their youngest was one-year old Janet. Every week my cousin Tomasa Moreno (Arturo's sister) and I would do our laundry at the spring inside BCE compound. We carried laundry on our heads and walked the distance. Doing laundry was a whole day event. We'd take our lunch to eat while the laundry dried on fences. I think what made it fun was that the laundry area had clear running water flowing around boulders and it was right across from the cassava mill. One day, when walking on a wooden plank bridge with a basin of laundry on my head, I slipped! No, I did not go in the water, but the load of wash went down. Suddenly, some of the men from the mill ran to the water and rescued whatever they could!

Our household was busy and happy. Although I had duties in the house, I mainly worked at the store attending to customers and keeping the books. Customers purchased goods mainly on credit so every payday at BCE, I would collect from them. I also went with Jovencia to Malabang and Cotabato on regular buying trips for supplies. The highway was closed, so we had to take the lansa (a ferry), the only transportation plying between Balabagan and Cotabato City. Later, Josephine, our sister from Padada joined the Hofer household and developed a thriving dressmaking business. Also, in a corner of the store, Andres gave rabies shots when he came home from work and I helped him by sterilizing needles. (The town did not have a health center.)

The business was not only a grocery store but it had also become a place for "Happy Hour." We sold Tanduay Rum and San Miguel Beer ("The best beer in the world!"). Besides having something to drink, customers enjoyed playing ping pong, visiting, and singing. It was a gathering place after work for BCE and other employees in the area.

At that time, there were four of us young ladies – Remy, Josephine, Tomasa, and me in the Hofer home. I remember the early morning serenades breaking the stillness of the night. Serenading is a lost culture now, but during our days, young men would sing in front of homes to woo the girls.

When I lived and worked in Balabagan, an opportunity opened up to attend Silliman University. In the spring of 1956, Dr. Roy and Edna Bell from Silliman University visited Malabang as part of their tour to visit alumni in Mindanao. Malabang was a target spot because there were already a number of alumni in the area: the Hofer brothers, Rev. Pionono Violanda, pastor of Malabang United Church of Christ, Earl Harpst of Puracan Coconut Plantation and several others who worked in the area. Vicente Hofer had been particularly close to the Bells when he was a student at Silliman before World War II.

Andres and Jovencia invited me and Josephine to the Silliman University Alumni reception for Dr. and Mrs. Bell. I listened to every word that Dr. Bell spoke from the podium and I observed the crowd throughout the evening. Oftentimes I had glanced at Mrs. Bell - an impeccably dressed, very lovely lady. Everybody was having a good time visiting and then she came to me, and said, "Hello Sweetie?"

What could I say? I was tongue-tied and my heart melted! She invited me to attend Silliman University, and when I told her that I would need work, she said she was going to arrange a work scholarship. It would be the fulfillment of a dream.

I was torn between my work at Jovencia's business and Silliman University, but the family, especially Jovencia, insisted that I must go, that they could take care of business. In my heart, however, there was a handsome gentleman with a good singing voice that I had fallen in love with. If I went, I would miss peeking through the window when he and his friends came to serenade. My parents were very happy, of course. I was glad and grateful for this opportunity to attend Silliman University. That opened a new chapter of my life.

To leave the security of a life in Balabagan was a major step, and as an eighteen-year old, I could only trust in God completely as I sailed into the unknown. He has always been my Pilot, and the Bible my compass. Vicente was so elated because his son, Hans was also going to Silliman. In fact, he designated himself as our escort.

A few months later, truckloads of our families and friends saw us off at Malabang Airport. It was my first airplane ride and it was an Otter Plane, a very small one. We flew to Iligan City in Lanao del Norte and I got very air sick. From Iligan, we took an inter-island boat. A full moon was just emerging on the horizon when the boat pulled out into the harbor. In those days single canvas cots were lined up in double rows in large spaces on the boat and one could see heads and bodies everywhere.

We arrived in Dumaguete just as the eastern skies had turned orange and blue. The boat docked in Looc, about a mile from Silliman University campus. Along the pier and the boulevard were lines of horse-drawn carts (tarnanilya), the only mode of public transportation in those days. Vicente engaged one of these carts to take us to the Park Hotel downtown. The tranquility of the city made the constant rhythmic sound of horses' hooves on paved streets more pronounced. What caught my attention immediately was a contraption underneath the horse' rear end – a diaper - to catch the poop. It was a city ordinance, the clerk said, to keep the city streets clean.

The following day, Mrs. Bell picked us up in her car and drove us on a tour of the campus. We went to the cafeteria for coffee and snacks. Vicente was beside himself, recalling how it was before the War - the same building, albeit food was now served on aluminum trays - remnants of Liberation from World War II. (I was too shy to ask what they used for plates or trays before the War.) He and Mrs. Bell were busy reminiscing about those old times. She left father and son at Doltz Hall where Hans was assigned a room and took me to Oriental Hall.

Underneath a canopy of purple bougainvillea at the entrance to the dormitory, stood a petite lady with hair in a bun and a broad welcoming smile! Mrs. Bell said to her, "Bebang, here is the girl from Mindanao I mentioned to you. I will pick her up tomorrow to take to Mr. Dato for her work scholarship."

"Bebang," turned out to be Mrs. Genoveva "Mommy" Espejo, matron of Oriental Hall (OH), a women's dormitory for

120 students in their sophomore year and above, including those in Graduate School and the College of Law. When I arrived, the freshmen dormitories were full, but a room on the ground floor of OH with four wooden bunk beds was designated for late freshmen girls. There were eight of us - definitely a minority - but that did not intimidate us.

Vicente stayed for a week. Hans and I shared our academic program with him. I enrolled in Business Administration and I showed him my work assignment in Townsend Memorial Student Center as an assistant. As a work student, I had to put in four hours of work a day, take full academic load and maintain a required grade point average. He was very concerned but I assured him that I would be fine. Being in a very new situation, I was grateful to Vicente for advising me. (He would play another role in my life years later.)

My dream to attend college was coming true and of all places, it was at Silliman University, far more than I had ever expected! I had waited and worked patiently and I was rewarded. Right before my very eyes a college education was starting to unfold. "The Lord is my Pilot and the Bible, my compass!"

CHAPTER 5

"For I know the plans I have for you....
They are plans for good and not for evil –
to give you a future and a hope."
(Jeremiah 29:11 TLB)

SILLIMAN UNIVERSITY

"Where the white sands and the corals, kiss the dark blue southern seas... Silliman beside the Sea!" These are some lyrics to the Alma Mater song of Silliman University, a campus by the sea in Dumaguete City, Negros Oriental. Founded by missionaries in 1901, this Presbyterian university has a reputation of quality among higher education institutions in the Philippines. At the gate of Oriental Hall, as I came out of Mrs. Bell's car, I could hardly believe that I was really there. I was amazed by the magnificent surroundings!

Success in college was within my grasp but it required total dedication to my studies. I adjusted well to a full academic load and working four hours a day as a work scholar. I chose Accounting as my major but my, oh my, how I struggled in those classes! However, I was determined to succeed and did well in all academic requirements and electives for a degree in Business Administration.

What I did not learn in the classroom, I learned on campus. Actually, the whole university was my classroom. Besides classes and work, I participated in extra-curricular activities: the Galilean Fellowship, the Christian Youth Fellowship (CYF), attended recitals; concerts; drama performances; oratorical contests; quiz bowls; debates, fine arts lectures by Prof. Albert Faurot; sang in the Silliman Church Covenant Choir; went to picnics; square dances and attended Silliman Church Sunday worship, vespers, and mid-week. I was Immersed in Silliman University life!

Our life in Oriental Hall was exciting, too. There were stringent dormitory "rules" to observe – study hour, visiting hours, required evening devotions and speaking English only. Learning to converse in English only was a top priority. But there were times for fun, too! I remember that towards the end of study hour, we would hear a vendor's voice outside, calling "botsada,"- fried taro root balls dipped in sugar – very delicious! We had one hour of break time, laughing, gossiping, snacking and then would go back to studying until lights out at 11:00. (However, some girls would stay in the hallways to play scrabble.)

At one time, what some of us had learned to enjoy most was an early morning swim near the boulevard and then stop in the cafeteria for breakfast on the way back to Oriental Hall. It was wonderful, until the cafeteria manager called Mrs. Espejo. "Bebang, there are wet chickens here and I do not like it. They are dripping wet from swimming and are here eating breakfast. " That was the end of our early morning swim near the boulevard!

Each of the 120 residents had to lead an evening devotion. I was petrified when I found   out, during my freshman year. What had saved me was each turn was in alphabetical order and "Tobias" was listed three months later. When my turn came, I was prepared! After that, two dorm mates asked to address me as "Big Sis" because they liked my devotion message. "OK," I told them. Soon other residents followed and I became a "Big Sis," even to their boyfriends. This nickname has stuck with me until now. We studied and lived together well, and in my senior year I was elected President of Oriental Hall.

When the director of Townsend Memorial Student Center where I worked quit, I asked for a transfer to Oriental Hall to be a desk assistant. This was approved and it started my long relationship with Oriental Hall Matron, Mrs. Espejo.

A FEROCIOUS STORM PAVED THE WAY

I completed my undergraduate program and earned my Bachelor in Business Administration degree in May 1960 with little fanfare as I was a "summerian" (a summer graduate). Although I didn't get a proper graduation ceremony, my heart was filled with joy and accomplishment, knowing I was the first in three generations of my family to attain a college education. I planned to return to Malabang and work in one of the American plantations there. I packed my belongings and waited for the boat. But a raging storm prevented inter-island vessels from coming to Dumaguete! I was stuck in Oriental Hall for a little longer. Mommy and I were the only ones left, for everybody else had gone home. I watched the cascading rain coming down the gutter behind the dormitory and I was imagining myself taking a shower under that warm rain water, when I heard Mommy Espejo's voice, "There is a call for you."

It was Dr. Robert Silliman, Executive Vice President! He said, "Come to my office. I want to talk to you."

I don't recall what I told him, but I ran to Mommy and asked her what she knew about the call. I had never talked to Dr. Silliman in all my four years at the University. I was petrified!

"Well, Dr. Silliman wants you to stay here and work with Pauline "Polly" Fitton as an assistant in the Dean of Women's office." I could not believe what I had just heard!

"But Mommy," I protested. "I want to go home. I am all packed and just waiting for the typhoon to pass and for the boat to come."

She sat me down and talked to me in earnest about working at Silliman. She reminded me of our past conversations and what I had said to her, that I would ask God to help me discern His will, and that "Where He wants me to go, I will go, and what He wants me to do I will do."

"Do you know that this is probably where God wants you to be?" She said.

"How can I do the job? My major is accounting and I did not even have a class in psychology?"

She said, "You will learn on the job and the Lord will guide you. Tomorrow, I will walk with you to Dr. Silliman's office."

The next day, the rain had stopped and there was no wind – a clear, bright day. Mommy met me in high heels, hair piled in a bun, face delicately-made up. With a twinkle in her eye, she said, "Let's go." I walked with her at a dizzying pace. She waited in the secretary's office while I went in to see Dr. Silliman for the first time in my life! What struck me immediately were his eye glasses riding on the lower bridge of his nose. A funny sight, I thought. A smile inside put me at ease and ready to listen to him. Come what may, I was ready.

In his gruff voice, he said, "We want you to stay and work as assistant to the Dean of Women, Polly Fitton. You are recommended strongly." I told him that accounting was my major. With eyes glowering at me above his glasses, he said, "So? For four years you have demonstrated your ability to work with students as a campus leader. You can do the job. Here, sign the contract."

Wow! One Hundred Fifty Pesos a month! It was more than I had ever expected. I thank him for this job offer, took the contract and promised to return it with my signature. The ensuing two days gave me a chance to assess my situation.

I decided to see Prof. Herbert Fitton, my dean in the School of Business Administration. He and his wife, Polly had made their home accessible to students, especially during holidays. I was usually one of those left on campus because it was too expensive to go home to Mindanao. So, I had developed a close relationship with this couple during college. Polly's appointment as Dean of Women occurred towards the end of my senior year, but I had never imagined that I might work with her. Prof. Fitton gave me reasons why I should stay.

He said, "We have watched and observed how you deal with students. You'll do just fine. You will find that working with people is more in your alley than working with figures in an accounting office."

I asked why he hadn't advised me to shift to another major.

He said, "You were too far into the program and shifting would have required another year at school. Sign the contract. You will enjoy working with Polly."

The following day, there was a knock on my door and Mommy announced, "We're leaving in an hour to go to Dr. Silliman's office." She had taken me under her wing to go through it all!

I signed the contract. There was a spring in my feet when I walked with Mommy this time. I saw the beauty of the campus in a way that I had never seen it before.

Who would have thought that a puny girl from Balabagan would be hired by Silliman University? Was this really where I should be? God's plan is definitely bigger than mine! I was so grateful for the opportunity to work immediately after college. I was at peace and felt a song in my heart.

The following day, I sent a telegram to my sister, Jovencia. The response was that the family could not believe Silliman University would offer me a job! They were joyous!

CHAPTER 6

"The Lord will guide you continually, and satisfy you with all good things,
and keep you healthy; you will be like a well-watered garden,
like an ever-flowing spring." (Isaiah 58:11 TLB)

A WELL-WATERED GARDEN

All education was interrupted during World War II, so I was the first one in my family to finish college. With my new job at Silliman University, I became the hope of my younger siblings and others in my family for college education. I took that responsibility seriously and with immense joy. I already felt like a "well-watered garden" with many blessings showered on me. I would share those blessings.

I plunged into my work as Assistant Dean of Women with confidence that I could do whatever it was that lay ahead. With a grateful heart, I embraced my work.

DEAN OF WOMEN'S OFFICE

The offices of Student Deans of Men and Women were in the Division of Student Personnel with Dr. Merton Munn as Head, and he was also the Dean of Instruction. He was on furlough in the summer of 1960 when the Acting Head recommended me as Assistant to the Dean of Women, Polly Fitton. When he returned that first semester, he questioned my appointment as my degree was in Business Administration. However, Polly Fitton told him, "Oh, Eufemia is great! She is fine working with me." Polly, who was very efficient and professional, had walked me through the ropes of my responsibilities and I had learned fast.

Student life is a vital part of the University. Polly explained to me that both Student Deans' offices worked together in all aspects of student life. Our main responsibilities included women's programs and women's dormitories but we worked with the Dean of Men's office on campus student organizations; awards convocation for outstanding campus student leaders; the Student Government on freshmen orientation; the Guidance Counselor on Student Resident Adviser program and with the Dormitory Management Council.

At one time, nearly half of Silliman University students lived on campus in regular and cooperative dormitories. Those were their "homes away from home" and the University therefore had to ensure a good and safe living environment. Each regular dormitory had a matron and a cooperative dormitory had an Adviser, who was a faculty or staff member.

SAMPAGUITA COTTAGE – A WOMEN'S COOPERATIVE DORMITORY

During my first year, in addition to my office duties, I was assigned as Adviser of Sampaguita Cottage, a women's cooperative dormitory, along with Ida Warner. Officers managed the daily aspect of cooperative dormitory life but Ida and I trained residents in menu planning, budgeting for food, marketing and housekeeping. A live-in cook did the marketing and she was assisted by residents in cooking.

The old thatched roof building with sawali (native material) walls was home to forty women. One large room had ten wooden double bunk beds for freshmen girls. Student Resident Advisers (SRA's) were assigned to them by the Guidance Counselor. Sophomore girls and upperclassmen occupied the other rooms. Ida and I occupied a tiny room with just walking space between our single beds. It opened into a small sitting room with large picture windows and a tiny wash basin in a corner. Mommy Espejo gave us three rattan lounge chairs from Oriental Hall. The cushions needed covers, so I sewed new ones from donated printed cotton feed sacks. A year later, Ida moved back to Oriental Hall as Mommy's assistant, and my younger sister, Rachel moved in with me. She was a freshman student in the College of Nursing.

Members of the Silliman University Board of Trustees took interest in our living conditions in the cooperative dormitories. Twice for lunch, we had Dra. Josefa Ilano, Chairman of the Board, and Mrs. Elsie Aguilar, a Board member. Joining residents at long tables and sitting on wooden benches, these two women displayed a grace and humility that left an indelible mark in my memory. They were impressed at the training that residents had in the cooperative dormitory.

In 1963, Rachel and I moved into a brand new two-storey Sampaguita. I served as Adviser of Sampaguita Cottage from 1960-1966 and through those years, the girls called me "Big Sis." When I resigned, Thelma Appleton said, "There will never be another 'Big Sis' on campus." However, the Tobias reign was not finished. Midway through her nursing program, Rachel had to change majors because of ill health, but she graduated in 1966 with a Bachelor of Arts degree in Anthropology. She was hired in the School of Music as a secretary and she took over my place as Adviser in Sampaguita Cottage. Our youngest sister, Fely enrolled at Silliman University at this time. Later, when Rachel left for the United States, Fely took over as Adviser. She had graduated that year with a Bachelor of Science degree in Arts and had been hired as secretary in the Home Economics Department. Altogether, there were nineteen years that Sampaguita Cottage had Tobias sisters as Advisers.

Six years as Assistant Dean of Women provided a rich opportunity for me to learn student personnel work. My mind was focused on my responsibilities and on advancing in my field – Student Personnel. I decided to study abroad. I perused catalogues of universities in the United States and I remember vividly reading the scholarship brochure of the American Association of University Women. (Years later, I became a member of AAUW.)

It happened! That year, Silliman University and the United Board for Christian Higher Education in Asia in New York picked me as one of two scholars to study abroad during the years 1966-1968. I was accepted at Syracuse University for a two-year program in Student Personnel. Upon completion, I would return to Silliman University to become its **First Filipino Dean of Women.** I was very, very excited!

The timing was perfect! Rachel had graduated and was working. She was helping Fely, our youngest sister, who had just started college. Abraham found work as a campus security guard at Silliman. Arturo graduated and worked in the Department of Psychology until his retirement. Ben, our youngest brother was on work scholarship, in the Silliman University College of Engineering. Upon his graduation with Bachelor of Science in Mechanical Engineering he joined the faculty of the College of Engineering. I had helped all my younger siblings through these years. "Big Sis" was ready to climb a new height!

CHAPTER 7

"In everything you do, put God first, and
He will direct you and crown your efforts with success."
(Proverbs 3:6 TLB)

ONE MORE RUNG TO CLIMB

Ten years at Silliman University as a student and as an Assistant Dean of Women paved the way for me to advance in my profession. The faculty and staff development plan of Silliman University included the training of Filipino staff to eventually take over positions held by fraternal workers (missionaries). In my case, I had served with two deans of women who were Americans. Through the United Board I was accepted into student personnel programs at both Denver University and at Syracuse University. I picked Syracuse. However, in the midst of preparation to go to Syracuse, something occurred that made me change lanes – destination still USA, but not as a student.

GENERAL EDUCATION AT SILLIMAN UNIVERSITY

Dr. Merton Munn, who was a Presbyterian missionary, sponsored by the United Board had arrived at Silliman University campus in May 1957 with his wife, Ila Smith Munn. The Munns readily enjoyed the hospitality of Silliman University and Dumaguete City. Some years later, Ila Munn passed away while serving Silliman University.

Dr. Munn had been appointed to develop the general education program at Silliman as recommended by the Fenn Survey of 1954-1955 – an objective assessment of University programs. In his positions as Dean of the College of Arts and Sciences and Dean of Instruction, he led the faculty in its development and he was the chief architect. "Silliman University General Education," as it was later known, was well underway when he became Vice-President for Academic Affairs in 1963.

In 1965, after nine years of service to Silliman University, Dr. Munn was recalled by the United Board to serve as Director of Research for the project, "Appraisal of Protestant Effort in Christian Higher Education in Asia." This position required his joining the United Board staff in New York City. He had enjoyed his work at Silliman and would have stayed on, but he was needed on the "Appraisal" project.

A FAREWELL TO SILLIMAN AND MARDI GRAS

Dr. Munn's last convocation on August 28, 1965 honored him for his service and it was also an official welcome to Dr. Paul Lauby as the new Vice-President for Academic Affairs. Dr. William P. Fenn, Executive Secretary of the United Board was also in attendance.

I did not attend the convocation that day in August. I was at the beauty shop in preparation for ushering at the University banquet that evening. My friend Lily Didal found me in Sampaguita Cottage later, and chided me for missing it as it was Dr. Munn's last convocation. He had delivered his farewell speech. Lily said, "Where have you been? Dr. Munn was looking for you."

"Why?" I asked. Lily replied that she did not know but, I told her, it could be about our Student Personnel exhibits in the Student Center.

My friends and I always ushered at banquets and took that work seriously. It is a lot of fun to dress well, greet guests at the entrance and to escort them to their tables - to see and to be seen. I reported to the banquet hall that night dressed in the traditional Philippine dress of "patadyong" (slim plaid skirt,) "kimona" (blouse) and with high heels and styled hair, I was ready! Wouldn't you know it? I was the only usher available when Dr. Munn arrived. Was it coincidence?

He asked, "Where were you this morning? I missed you. "

I told him that I had to finish our Student Personnel display, which was true; I could not tell him that I also went to the beauty shop. I apologized for my absence and at the head table, I said, "Here you are, Sir." We stood by the table momentarily and he said, "Why don't you sit here with me?"

"Oh no, not tonight" I said, "Maybe someday!" Another guest came but he turned to me, "I'll see you after the banquet. Don't run away."

"There will be lots of people who would like to talk to you."I protested.

"Well, then how about taking me around the Mardi Gras?" He said. I was a little surprised.

The Mardi Gras was organized by the "College Y" and other campus organizations. A carnival-like event, it had booths with different displays lined up in the Quadrangle.

"Oh, yes, I can meet you at the Mardi Gras." I left and continued escorting guests to their tables. Who would not want to take the Academic Vice President around? It would be a privilege and an honor!

The campus organizations had done a marvelous job of planning and organizing. Booths were very well organized with interesting displays. I took Dr. Munn to different booths. Then we joined some friends and enjoyed the rest of the evening chatting and drinking warm Coca Cola (Refrigeration was still a luxury in those days).

In the next few days he invited me again: first to Al Mar, the famous restaurant by the sea, then to a movie – "Battle of the Bulge" - and finally to a pancake breakfast in his home. He took the time to explain that pancakes are common American breakfast. At the last dinner, again at Al Mar's, we were seated by a window overlooking the ocean. A breeze cooled off a warm September night. A crescent moon appeared and he said, "Oh, it is a wet crescent moon." I did not know until then that one can predict whether it will be dry or rainy weather, according to the shape of the crescent moon.

I was greatly innocent about these invitations. I thought that he just needed someone to talk to or to listen to him talk about Silliman, the Philippines, people, culture, his new job at the United Board and my going to Syracuse University. He took so much time to talk that he hardly touched his chicken dinner. Something was going on.

Through the years, I had admired Dr. Munn very much as an administrator. His extra attention and the special times we were having together were very unusual and I began to wonder about them myself. I was in the lane leading to Syracuse University, but the events of that week made me think seriously that I might have to change lanes. A kiss under the umbrella on a rainy night sealed my fate. He left on September 2, 1965.

Letters from Dr. Munn in New York poured in. He agonized over the course of our personal events because he was ultimately responsible in recommending me to the United Board for a scholarship. For that, he had considered my professional advancement and my future service to Silliman University. Those months were extremely difficult for me, too. I continued pursuing my plans to go to Syracuse but he had sounded serious in his plans for our life together. In the end, on bended knee I submitted it to God and again, I said, "Where you want me to go, I will go and what you want me to do, I will do." "The Lord is my Pilot and the Bible is my compass."

By December, three months after Dr. Munn left, I had to have a very serious conversation with Paul Lauby. I told him to start a search for another Filipino Dean of Women because it was not going to be me. My destination was still the USA but not to Syracuse. Paul just smiled when I said, "We make our plans, but God has a bigger and better plan." He understood, and he said he had predicted that things would turn out differently than planned. Even Dr. Fenn, who came on a special project to Silliman University and had brought a package to me from Dr. Munn said, "I will see you in New York." He and Dr. Munn had started to work on the "Appraisal" project.

ENGAGEMENT IN THE SHADOW OF A FAN PALM

To do the observations for his project, Dr. Munn had consultation trips to three countries including the Philippines. He took a vacation from visiting schools in the Philippines and spent a week at Silliman. In the shadow of a fan palm in "DYSR Camp Seasite," a few kilometers south of Dumaguete, I made a decision that changed my life forever. I got engaged to Dr. Merton Munn.

Our engagement came as a great surprise to the Silliman University community. Who would not be surprised? So was I!

Who was I? What was I? Was it a coincidence that a ferocious storm had kept me at Silliman in June 1960 and had led me to sign a job contract? Or was it my destiny?

After we married, I asked Mert "why me?" He said that he was drawn to my Christian personality and had observed my ways in dealing with people. But I began to remember long conversations when he'd stopped in my office after work. I remembered our walks after lunch back to the office. He would be by Arts and Sciences building when I'd come by from Sampaguita Cottage and we would walk the long corridor through the College of Law down to my office in Guy Hall, and he would proceed to the Administration building. Following our engagement, the next few months rolled along with drastic changes in my preparation for the future, a turn of events that made my family very happy!

In June 1966, ten years after I had arrived at Silliman, a cable came from Dr. Munn in New York City: "August is my vacation. Let us get married."

My resignation from Silliman University was effective July, 1966. (The University found Atty. Mercedes Gomez to take over as dean of women when Thelma Appleton's term terminated, so Mrs. Gomez became the first Filipino Dean of Women.)

Then, I had to say goodbye to a campus that had been my home for ten years. Fond memories remain with me. I had enjoyed singing in the Covenant Choir, swimming at Silliman Farm, and eating "puto maya" (sticky rice cooked in coconut milk) with chocolate in the market place. I had chaperoned many college dances, class picnics and I had been a Co-Adviser of the ROTC Corps of Sponsors. Single faculty and staff had organized YAG, the Young Adults Group. We went to fiestas and played Rook (a card game) in different homes and we sponsored the Dauin United Church of Christ. Periodically we'd spend a day cleaning up or attending Sunday worship service together. Lasting friendships were developed in those years. Now, a new chapter was unfolding and it was outside the confines of Silliman University.

HOMETOWN WEDDING AND HONEYMOON IN HONG KONG

Our wedding on August 21, 1966 in Malabang, Lanao del Sur was a great gift that I could give to my family and friends, most of whom were homesteaders as my parents were in the 1930's. To see one of their own succeed at Silliman and come home ten years later to get married to someone very special from Silliman and then go to live in New York City was beyond their imagination! The community was happy and proud.

I chose Malabang United Church of Christ with thatch roof, dirt floor, sawali walls, and plain wooden pews. It was starkly different from Silliman Church, but it was my church of choice to remind me of my roots and to honor my family and the people in my community.

My sister Jovencia and my parents arranged everything. When I arrived three days before, the wedding cake had already come from the Country Bake Shop in Manila, courtesy of its owner, Dra. Josefa Ilano, Chairman of Silliman University Board of Trustees. Jovencia was nervous that the groom would be coming all the way from New York! How could he make it? I told her to camp at the RCPI, the telegraph office, to wait for Mert's cable from Manila. She did, and the cable said,

"Arrive Malabang August 20." Just a day before our wedding!

Mert had to secure a permit from the US Embassy and it was a holiday when he had arrived Manila. He got it in time to fly to Dumaguete City to join Rev. Fred Appleton, pastor of Silliman Church and his wife Thelma. The next day they flew to Malabang with my sister, Rachel, my brother, Ben, my cousin Arturo and dear friend Paquita Josue. Gideon Alegado, Rachel's special friend had already arrived from Gingoog Christian College where he was teaching. Thelma brought orchids from Dumaguete and made my wedding bouquet. Mrs. Maria Clara Lobregat offered the use of her brand new guest house on the Balabagan Coconut Estate (BCE) for the Appleton's and Mert.

The wedding ceremony was performed by Rev. Pionono Violanda, a graduate of Silliman University School of Divinity. Our sponsors were Mrs. Lobregat and Vicente Hofer, who had escorted me to Silliman ten years before. Mert's best man was Fred Appleton. My bridesmaid was my sister, Rachel. Paquita Josue sang and my father gave me away. It was a wonderful, simple wedding ceremony, just as I had wanted. Mert did say later that he had never knelt so long on very hard floor!

The wedding reception was at the Sultan Hotel, operated by Earl Harpst, a former student at Silliman School of Business Administration. Guests included Silliman alumni and many close friends of my family. It was a joyous day, especially for Jovencia, who had pressed me on to go to Silliman and to my parents.

Interestingly, a few guests did not attend in protest of Mrs. Lobregat's entering a Protestant church. She was Catholic and employees of BCE worshipped in the Catholic parish church right on her plantation. However, she wanted to show those people that it was time for Catholics and Protestants to reach a common ground. Little did I know then that our wedding would be the start of bridging the gap between Catholics and Protestants in Balabagan.

The next day, Mert and I flew to Hong Kong for our honeymoon. Hong Kong was one of his favorite cities in Asia. For one who had not even been to Manila, this was a big leap, but it was only the beginning of years and years of travel.

We stayed at the Fortuna Hotel on Nathan Road in Kowloon. Mert was an excellent tour guide, having visited Hong Kong a number of times before. We took the Star Ferry across Hong Kong harbor, and a tram up to Victoria Peak for an afternoon tea or dinner at twilight. I loved the boat rides to floating restaurants and eating fish picked from the fresh fish tank. These were all new to me. Shopping on Kowloon sidewalks was fun. Then a bus tour took us to the "New Territories," a tourist spot on the border between Hong Kong and mainland China. At that time, it was a vast expanse of simple hamlets and rice paddies. (Now it is the city of Shenzhen, a major business and financial center in Guangdong province.)

After our honeymoon, we returned to Silliman University. I stayed there while Mert went to India and Thailand for Ford Foundation conferences. He also found a good location for what is now Payap University in Cheng Mai. The United Board by that time had appointed me as his secretary and in his absence I began transcribing tapes of his meetings in different countries. He came home for Christmas but left for Pakistan shortly thereafter.

Then, in February 1967, I met him in Hong Kong on a very cold winter day. We were about to start our new life.

CHAPTER 8

"Fear not for I am with you.........I will strengthen you.
I will help you; I will uphold you with my victorious right hand."
(Isaiah 41:10 TLB)

NEW BEGINNING: UNCHARTED WATERS

I left Manila on a hot and humid afternoon in February 1967 with a trustful heart. The direction of my life was changing completely. After just a few hours I disembarked in Kaitak Airport in Hong Kong. It was very cold! An icy wind from the harbor whipped against my face as I was holding the handrail tightly while searching the crowd for Mert. There he was! On his arm was my teal wool winter coat, which we had ordered during our honeymoon a few months before.

The United Board project – "Appraisal of Protestant Effort in Higher Education in Asia," was having meetings in Hong Kong. Serving with him on the international team were Dr. William "Bill" Fenn, Executive Secretary of the United Board and Dr. Hachiro Yuasa, former president of International Christian University (ICU) in Tokyo. Each country in the project had its own local team. As we traveled, meetings were recorded on tapes and it was my job to transcribe them – while "on the road" – on a portable typewriter.

The team's next meetings were at Soochow University in Taipei, Taiwan. I did not have to attend meetings, so I had some free time. The wives of faculty members gave me a tour of the city and took me to lunch in a very elegant hotel in Taipei where forks and spoons were in silver and chopsticks were in ivory. After sessions at the University, Mert and I walked and soaked in the beauty of Yangmingsan Park and toured the Palace Museum.

We took the train to Taichung in the south to visit Tunghai Christian University. On the train we were served lunch of stir fry vegetables and rice. Mert looked at his lunch and asked, "What shall I do with this?" I handed him a pair of chopsticks, and Bill said, with a big smile, "Eat it." He probably wished he had a hamburger!

At Tunghai University, we stayed in the Guest House. The place did not have central heating, so it was too cold to do any typing but the hostess came periodically with hot wet towels and helped me rub my hands. Breakfast was usually congee (rice porridge) and we learned from Bill to sprinkle different condiments – chopped meat, shrimp and soy sauce on it. I loved it!

En route to the United States from Taiwan, Mert and I spent a week of vacation in Tokyo, Japan. There we also visited Bing Calderon, daughter of Silliman University President Cicero Calderon; she was a student at International Christian University. The hotel clerk offered to call a taxi, but Mert insisted doing it on his own. Down the street we went. He hailed a taxi and told the driver where to take us. The driver responded with a blank look despite Mert's use of hand gestures.

Finally I said, "You want me to try?" I spoke a few words, and off we went! Mert was astonished!

"What did you say?" he asked. "I told him to take us to ICU." I said.

"It was in Japanese! Where did you learn that?" "From Dr. Yuasa," I told him.

You see, during meals I sat between Mert and Dr. Yuasa or Bill, so I learned some Japanese from Dr. Yuasa, who very kindly taught me basic words and phrases.

I enjoyed Tokyo, but soon we left on a Northwest Orient Airlines flight to the USA. I had the long hours to take stock of my new life.

We arrived at SEATAC – Seattle-Tacoma Airport -- on March 7, 1967. I had jet lag. I have no recollection of what I saw but I remember we ate in a Chinese restaurant with Mert's daughter Gwen and Len, his son-in-law, who were so gracious. I was immediately taken by nine-year old Doug, the only grandson. Doug and his sisters, Debbie, Linda and Teri were so happy to see "Gramps." Mert's daughter, Evelyn and baby granddaughter, Lisa were there, too. If I was apprehensive before, upon my introduction to his "family" my fears quickly receded. This was a warm, loving family and I was now a big part of it.

We took a week to drive across the country from Seattle to New York City. What an amazing introduction to the sights and sounds of the USA! It was like a dream. How could a simple girl from Balabagan be traveling through the heart of America? In the back of my mind I was wondering if there were any leeches in the thick forest I saw. On the way we visited his brothers and parents in Wisconsin and Michigan. His parents had retired to Hillsdale, Michigan, near Mert's brother, Dr. Harold Munn, Dean of Hillsdale College.

When we arrived in New York City, I looked in total amazement! It definitely was a new beginning for me - no longer would I be walking in the shadows of acacia trees but in the shadows of giant buildings; no longer seeing the Pacific Ocean, but the Hudson River and on the other side, New Jersey.

THE UNITED BOARD FOR CHRISTIAN HIGHER EDUCATION IN ASIA

Our apartment in Morningside Gardens was on the third floor of one of the high-rise buildings on 123rd and Broadway in the upper west side of Manhattan. It was an easy walking distance to work through Barnard College. There, I had my first cultural shock – boys and girls kissing each other in broad daylight! Where I came from even holding hands was nearly a taboo, except in secret.

The United Board offices were on the 12th floor of the Interchurch Center at 475 Riverside Drive. Our office had a good view of the Hudson River. The staff had prepared a welcome reception for us. Everyone's eyes were on me, wondering why Mert had to cross the Pacific Ocean to get a bride, when there were single ladies among them. Being an "Asian" married to an American was not a common sight in those days. I was conscious of the typical stereotypes, but I put this back in my mind and concentrated on adjusting to the new environment and the people. I found them very friendly and curious about the Philippines. The confidence I had developed from my training and working at Silliman University, and having read "How to Win Friends and Influence People" by Dale Carnegie, prepared me for this sudden change in my life. I was introduced to all the United Board personnel, including Mrs. Elizabeth Luce Moore, the president. I was happy to see Bill Fenn, of course, with whom we had traveled in Hong Kong and Taiwan.

It took time for me to get used to riding the elevator with people who were so tall and big! There had been no elevators where I was from. Each tIme I walked in, I had to find a corner but people were wonderful and gave me a spot so I wouldn't be squeezed.

It took me quite a while to get used to American food. Pink hamburger I could never eat and a huge pile of pancakes on a platter was much too much! We ate lunch in the Interchurch cafeteria. My usual order for months was a doughnut and a hotdog smothered with chili. I looked forward to Thursdays because Bill designated it as Chinese food day and we walked to his favorite Chinese restaurant up the hill. Eventually, I developed a taste for well done grilled steak, baked potato, and green salad when we ate in a restaurant. I cooked Filipino food in our apartment, especially when we had dinner guests.

Mert and I attended Riverside Church for Sunday and mid-week services. I had to pinch myself sitting in a pew in this fabulous church with magnificent choir and half a dozen ministers! It was within walking distance of our apartment but occasionally we went to a Presbyterian Church downtown. Once, we attended Marble Collegiate Church and heard Dr. Norman Vincent Peale. From then on I had become a student of Dr. Peale's "Power of Positive Thinking," and it has had an immense impact on my life all these years.

I loved New York! A friend who served on the City Arts Commission gave us complimentary tickets to Carnegie Hall, Philharmonic Hall and Town Hall. In the summer we had picnic suppers in Central Park while waiting for the De La Corte Theater to open for an evening of Shakespeare. I liked plays on Broadway,

New Year's Eve in Time Square and so many other things to see and do there. We took in the best that the city could offer.

We rode the subway in the city all the time but used our car to see farther places. I especially remember touring the Northeast during fall with the tree leaves bursting with color. My world expanded with trips to Niagara Falls, Toronto, Canada, to West Point Academy, Washington, D.C. and other not-so-far sights while we lived in New York.

When Mert was gone on "Appraisal" trips to Asia, I often walked to work with one of the United Board office secretaries, who lived in the same high-rise we were in. When he was in India for forty-four days, Dr. Albert and Edna Sanders, our neighbors and long time missionaries in the Philippines, took me under their wings. On my birthday, he delivered a huge bouquet of flowers that Mert had asked him to order. We also knew Arthur Carson, who had been president of Silliman University, and his wife Edith. Dinner with these two couples had always been occasions to reminisce about our years in the Philippines.

Mert came home from India in time for Thanksgiving, and the first thing we did was buy a 22- pound turkey. The words "dressed" and "dressing" in reference to turkey fixings were new in my vocabulary. Mert asked the grocer how much dressing to put in the dressed turkey. By that time, my mind embraced this experience with humor, but I was still a bit confused about "dressed" and "dressing." Papa raised turkey on our farm, but we never "dressed" a turkey. The grocer asked, "How many are there to eat?"

"There are two of us," Mert answered. The grocer could not believe – a 22 lb. turkey for two. I just smiled.

Preparing that dressed turkey with dressing to stuff inside its cavity and baking it for hours was an experience I'd never forget! We feasted on that bird for three months mostly in sandwiches and soups! I also discovered how to make curried turkey.

My life in New York was cluttered with all kinds of things to see and learn but I also enjoyed my work which took me to eleven countries in Asia - by listening to hundreds of voices on tapes. Mert and I wrote reports on 84 colleges and universities in those eleven Asian countries. I knew the names of all the administrators, and could put faces to the names which had been a great pleasure at the final Conference in Hong Kong.

There, at one of our small lunches, I sat between Bill and Mert and ordered pancakes! Believe it or not, I had learned to love pancakes in the short time that I lived in New York City. Midway through the meal of Chinese dishes, came my order in an elegant covered dish. The waiter opened it, and there it was a lonely, tiny, thin pancake! Mert grinned but Bill said, "Never order pancake in a Chinese restaurant." I asked why he did not tell me when I did, he said, "Because I wanted you to see it." I have never forgotten that!

After the "Appraisal" conference, Mert was offered the vice-chancellor's position at Chung Chi College in the University of Hong Kong. It was a good administrative position, but this University did not offer an opportunity for advanced education for me. So, he chose to return to Whitworth College in Spokane, Washington, where he had been Dean and I could continue my education.

WHITWORTH COLLEGE

We left New York City on January 28, 1969 to drive to Spokane. It was a blustery day. Ice floes clogged the Hudson River and news of bad roads westward was rampant. Spokane's temperature dipped to 25 degrees below zero the day of our departure. The Carsons and Sanders saw us off with food for the road.

In all my time growing up in the Philippines I had never seen snow, of course, until now, but we loved to sing 'I'm Dreaming of a White Christmas." Driving nearly 3,000 miles west in the dead of winter was definitely daunting but we drove on, stopping every night before sundown. In Nebraska, we stopped at Hastings College, where Mert's friend, Dr. Theron "Ted" Maxson was President. Ted and his wife Eleanor were summer neighbors at Deer Lake, north of Spokane, where Mert had built a small rustic cabin. It was snowing profusely when we left Hastings but when we got to Lincoln City, the freeway was clear. To see cars in ditches was not for the faint of heart, but we managed to miss the worst of the weather.

When we arrived, Spokane was deeply entrenched in snow and Whitworth College' (now Whitworth University) breathtaking campus filled with the tallest pine trees was a winter wonderland. Mert signed a contract for five years – 1969-1974. He became the Head of the Education Department and concurrently Director of the Evening School. I was hired as Secretary-Receptionist in the Admissions Office. I enjoyed my job but then, I discovered that I could take classes, paying no tuition because I was a faculty wife. With Mert's counsel, I made a career change from *Higher Education Administration to Public Elementary and Secondary Education: Teaching and Administration.*

I started in the Evening School to get my teaching credentials by taking elementary methods classes. Eventually, I resigned from my job when I decided to work on my master's degree as well.

To fulfill a requirement in one of my methods classes, I had to volunteer and observe a second grade classroom. One cute little guy, Kenny kept following me all day. Finally, he asked, "How old are you?"

"I am sure I am older than your mom. How old is she?" I asked.

"Oh, my mom is very old – 25 years old." He looked at me up and down and said, "Chinese don't grow old, huh."

"I am a Filipino," I told him.

Later, I met his mom who was tall and fairly large. In Kenny's young mind, age had something to do with body size and height. The innocence of children in their formative years! Right then, I made the right decision to shift from higher education to elementary to work with children.

In 1970, while I was working on my Teaching Certificate at Whitworth, I became a citizen of the United States. Two years later, I earned my Master's degree in Education and in 1984, my Principal's Certificate. Both certificates – for teaching and for administration – were for elementary and secondary level. I was poised for a new career adventure. Another new beginning!

LAKELAND VILLAGE SCHOOL

One day in 1973, a friend, whose husband was on the Whitworth faculty, invited me to Lakeland Village where she was a speech therapist. Lakeland Village at that time was a residential institution for 1000 adults and children with developmental disabilities. She introduced me to the director of Vocational Education, who took the time to give me a tour. All the residents had different kinds of disability but 200 of these were young people who were being trained in vocational skills. They worked as "details" in different locations on campus. At the end of the tour, he offered me a job as an "Institutional Teacher," to teach math and reading. I was stunned! But I took the job.

I enjoyed teaching math and reading in the Vocational Department. A few months later, however, Dr. Jack Bratten, Head of the Psychology Department, asked me to develop a pilot program for school-age residents, who were not admitted in public schools because of severe and profound disabilities. They were classified as "non-trainable and non-educable."

The new assignment was happening because Washington State had passed a bill to provide education for all children, regardless of disabilities. Shortly thereafter, "Education for All" was signed into Law by President Gerard Ford. Lakeland Village had to come up with an education and training program for them. This was a new thrust in education, long before colleges and universities had special education classes!

I asked Dr. Bratten, "Where do I begin and how?"

"I don't know. Start from scratch," he said. I told him to give me six weeks.

It may seem impossible for one person with no preparation in special education to develop a program within that time frame but we were fortunate that Lakeland Village had a very good County Library. I asked Edith, the librarian to collect books for my research and she was a big help! I also requested that Kathy Kipp, who had just graduated from college with a degree in psychology, assist me in the project.

Kathy and I took one living unit – Birch Hall-- where there were 12 children who were non-verbal, non-ambulatory, deaf and blind. They were totally dependent on attendant counselors for their daily living. With daily observations, interviews with Birch Hall staff and research from books, we came up with areas to train the children to become able to function independently: communicating, dressing, eating, toileting, developing mobility, dexterity and some prevocational skills.

Dr. Bratten was amazed when I presented the "Pilot Program," after six weeks.

"There is a big catch," I told him. In order for the program to succeed, it would require a major shift from custodial care – attendant counselors doing everything for residents – to training the residents to do the work themselves, for example, dressing and eating. It was a drastic change! It required more than a few meetings with living unit managers and attendant counselors with lots of modeling to attendant counselors how to teach and train the children. Amazingly, it worked!

The Lakeland Village Pilot Program was well underway in March 1975 when I resigned for another beginning into uncharted waters.

CHAPTER 9

"If you give, you will get! Your gift will return to you in full and
overflowing measure,
pressed down, shaken together to make room for more and running
over.
Whatever measure you use to give –large or small—
Will be used to measure what is given back to you."
(Luke 6:38)

TO ALASKA AND BACK

Spring of 1974 was a very busy time for us. Mert's retirement from Whitworth College in May coincided with the opening of Spokane EXPO '74. In addition, Whitworth conferred an honorary doctorate on President Quintin "King" Salas Doromal of Silliman University. Mert had known King when he was in administration at Silliman. Whitworth President Edward Lindaman and his wife, Gerrie visited Manila when Ed was president of Presbyterian Men and were hosted by King and his wife, Pearl. We were honored to have the Doromals as our guests in our home when they were in Spokane for the ceremony.

I continued teaching at Lakeland Village despite the constant flow of guests in our Spokane home and on our cabin in Deer Lake. Then, when EXPO ended in September 1974, my sister Rachel and her husband, Gideon Alegado arrived from Silliman University to start their graduate program at Oregon State University (OSU) in Corvallis, Oregon. A year later my brother Ben would also arrive. Shortly thereafter his wife Laraine and their young son Chris would follow. Ben and Laraine had also been accepted to attend OSU for their graduate studies. (Through the years, the Alegado children - G-mer and Garnet and Tobias's boys Chris and Julius filled our home with joy and laughter.)

Just after we got the Alegado's settled, the Board of Trustees of Sheldon Jackson College in Sitka, Alaska, asked if they could appoint Mert as "Interim President" to commence as soon as possible. I was not surprised at all! Mert's outstanding record as a college and university administrator and his close association and work with the Presbyterian Church made him a prime candidate. Together, we made the decision for him to answer the call. We worked as a team and we were always open to where our services could make a difference. He was told that the president of Sheldon Jackson College had to resign and Mert's leadership was needed. We were both excited that he would end his academic career as president of a college.

Mert flew to Alaska that November and assumed the presidency of Sheldon Jackson College. He came home to Spokane for Christmas, which we celebrated with Gideon and Rachel – their first Christmas in the USA. It was wonderful to have family and together, we discussed our immediate future. I had already considered resigning from my teaching job at Lakeland Village but living in Alaska would mean living quite far from Oregon. Rachel and Gideon assured us that they would be fine. They were going to be busy with adjustment to Oregon State and their academic work anyway.

In January 1975 I visited Mert in Sitka when Sheldon Jackson College Board of Trustees met. At a community banquet, seated to my left was Dr. Robert "Bob"Lodwick, United Board president and Presbyterian Church (USA) ex-officio member of SJC Board. We knew him when we were working with United Board in New York.

Bob said, "Femme, whatever you are doing in Spokane, you may have to quit and come to Sitka. You will be an asset to SJC and a tremendous help to Mert."

"Oh, I thought it was an interim position," I told Bob.

"Not just interim," Bob said. "The Board decided to make his position permanent for a period of three years. Mert has not had a chance to tell you yet because we just came from that meeting."

I told Bob that I had already decided to resign from teaching and come to Sitka. (In the next three years, Bob continued to come for Board meetings and was very pleased at SJC's progress.)

So I resigned from Lakeland Village in March 1975. Mert came home and I traveled with him to Alaska on the ferry "Columbia" from Seattle through the Inside Passage to Sitka.

SHELDON JACKSON COLLEGE

Sitka is on Baranof Island in Southeast Alaska. Sheldon Jackson College was one of eight "ethnic schools" of the Presbyterian Church (USA), founded by Dr. Sheldon Jackson, a Presbyterian missionary to Alaska. Decades before, it had been a boarding school for American Indians and Eskimos. Through the years, it had expanded to include college level programs. When I was there, most of the students were Alaska Native Americans and Eskimos from villages as far away as Point Barrow in the North and they lived in dormitories on campus. There were a few Caucasian students from "the Lower 48," who chose to attend for cultural immersion.

I taught remedial math and reading, and volunteered in the SJC Museum of Native American Artifacts, but I gave top priority to being the official hostess of the college. Mert and I discussed this aspect of my work and we both decided to open our home for entertaining. The president's home sits on a knoll and had a breath-taking view of Sitka Harbor.

We loved to entertain. Every Friday night we had a sit-down dinner for eight and we hosted receptions periodically. And there were unscheduled lunches or dinners for out-of-town guests. Thursday night was arts and crafts for native wood carving and bead work. Twice a year SJC Board meeting was followed by a sit-down dinner in the president's home.

Mert told me early on that any entertaining we did had to come out of our pocket. I assured him not to worry and that I was resourceful. People at the college introduced us to fishing from the tide flats especially for salmon, picking huckleberries and digging clams, each according to their season. Large clams were ground for chowder or baked in half shell as an appetizer. I gathered fiddle heads (emerging ferns) on hillsides, the same variety that we have in the Philippines, which were excellent for salad. Armed with cowbells tied to my waist to warn bears in logging areas, I picked huckleberries which were good for desserts and jam. I loved these outdoor adventures! SJC faculty, who were also engaged in commercial fishing, supplied us with 25-pounder salmon. I bought blocks of frozen Dungeness crab meat from the cannery. In a small island city of 2, 000 people, word easily got around that this Filipino wife of SJC president did a lot of cooking. In fact, one day when the cannery was closed and I needed crab, a boat had just come in and some of the crew gave their take-home crabs to me.

When Mert came home and saw those crabs scrambling out of the buckets, he said "Oh my, now what are you going to do with those?" "Cook them and eat them," I replied. I used those for leisurely eating but for crab shortcake, I used frozen crab meat. The recipe calls for lightly sautéed crab meat smothered in white sauce and poured over hot biscuits - easy to fix on short notice. And it was not unusual that he'd call and ask, "What's for lunch? Three people just arrived on the plane."

"Grilled salmon fillet or crab shortcakes," I'd reply.

"Can we have both? I am sure these folks from New York would enjoy both."

"Sure, just give me one hour to get them ready." I said. Dessert was huckleberry pie.

Alice Postell, Sheldon Jackson College Museum curator, arranged a reception for forty museum curators, who were on an Alaska cruise after a conference in Seattle. She asked me to serve lemon meringue pie.

"I have never baked lemon meringue pie in my life," I told her. "Huckleberry pie is good."

"Oh no, that will make their teeth blue," she replied.

Well, Alice and I compromised. I baked twelve of each – huckleberry and lemon meringue. Mert came home for lunch and saw my pies! I told him with a big grin that the "lips" of my meringue pie were all in different shapes and lopsided. We laughed, and he said, "It will not matter when it is cut." He was right! To Alice's chagrin, the guests preferred the huckleberry pie! (We ended up giving away half a dozen meringue pies to dormitory residents. They loved them.)

75

Dr. Charles "Chuck" Bovee, the academic dean, and his wife Edie were just as busy entertaining out-of-town guests as we were. One time, Edie's call sounded so frantic, "Come, can you come immediately? There is a live something coming out of the fridge."

It was an octopus that her son, Ken, who worked for Fish and Game, had brought home. The fridge had been too cold and tentacles started to squirm out of the container which scared Edie! I took the critter back to my house and cooked it. Late that afternoon, she called again, to ask us to join them for dinner with guests who just arrived on the ferry.

"Sure, what do you want me to bring? I asked.

"Oh, anything that is easy to fix," she replied. Chuck and Edie were gracious hosts and offered an array of salmon and crab. The dish I brought was just little bit different. When I helped Edie clear the kitchen, she asked,

"What was that you brought? It tasted so good." I wished she had not asked, but I had to tell her.

"I am glad you liked it. It was the octopus you gave me this morning." Edie just about dropped the empty dishes she had in her hands!

My life in Sitka was not just all food and entertaining. I had serious responsibilities as well. Upon my arrival in Sheldon Jackson College, Mert asked me to bridge the gap between SJC with both the Native Americans and the Japanese. Native Americans held demonstration classes in word carving, silver jewelry making and bead work at the Visitors Center in Sitka Park. The Japanese operated a pulp mill in Sitka.

"How do I bridge the gap?" I asked.

"Do whatever you can to cultivate relationships with these groups." He said.

Soon I saw an opportunity. I asked, "So are you free Wednesday after work?"

"No, there is a faculty meeting," he said.

"Well, you may have to postpone it. There is a funeral for an Indian chief in the Presbyterian Church. I am going." Well, Mert with SJC faculty and staff attended. It paved the way for a positive relationship and led to SJC's designating a Native American Day. For this day, the Southeast Alaska Indian tribes conduct a Powwow on campus. One event, I recall, was the "money blanket dance." An announcer calls a group or a name, to dance around a blanket on the floor with dollar bills in hand to drop as a donation when the drumming stops.

"Mrs. Munn, that's you; get up there and dance," my seatmate said. So, I danced to the rhythm of the drums, the loud drumming seemed endless; then suddenly it stopped. I dropped the dollar bills on the blanket and returned to my seat.

In no time, a tall Indian chief in his royal regalia glowered at me and in his deep voice, "What tribe are you from? I have not seen you before. You danced very well."

I told him I was a Filipino and that I was the wife of President Munn. But I look like a native!

"Oh, that is very nice," he said. With a broad smile, he shook my hand.

Then in the Visitors Center, I learned to do Tlingit bead work under Mrs. Esther Littlefield, who became a very dear friend. She and Charlie, her husband, would come to our home for dinner; likewise we would eat with them. She gave Mert many of her designs which he later used for his wood carvings, and I learned Tlingit Indian culture.

I loved the outdoors and tried to live in it like the Indians did. During herring season, they took me to the shore to gather herring eggs using branches and twigs of a certain tree spread on the shore. I had forgotten who gave me a herring net – a contraption to lower and tie between moorage of two boats in the dock. I did this at night and harvested herring in the morning - anywhere from 100 to 200 little fish! What a catch! I took salted or dried herring to my family in Oregon. Fishing for pink salmon from tide flats was my favorite. Once, I caught my 7 fish limit weighing anywhere from 3 to 7 pounds each. I hauled the heavy bag to the car and drove off quickly. I got home and there was no reel! It was a gift from Mert! I had to retrieve it, and there it was in the parking lot, all smashed into pieces. In my haste, I had driven over it.

The Sitka Pulp Mill was operated by the Japanese as part of the Marshall Plan agreement after World War II. It brought in a contingent of Japanese families to Sitka. I met one Japanese lady in the fabric shop, one day, and we talked about fabrics. She asked what I was doing and I told her I was at Sheldon Jackson College. I had to buy fabric for maternity dresses that I wanted to make for a pregnant Eskimo student. The lady's husband was the manager of the pulp mill. She said she taught Japanese flower-making and invited me to her home. There I met women who were enrolled in her class; some were Japanese, so, I enrolled in her flower-making class. All materials for flowers and tools came from Japan. I made roses, iris, tiger lilies, poppies, and daises. I still have the flowers, decades later. This started a bridge with the Japanese, and soon we had Japanese guests in our home for social functions.

Once, Mert and I were guests of the Consul of Japan at a reception on board a Japanese Navy Ship that came to Sitka Harbor. The captain voiced his concern to Mert when he saw me with a glass of "sake." Mert assured the captain that I could handle it. Years before he had taught me how to drink it – just to pretend to take a sip—a skill which would serve me well many times, afterwards.

The teaching, the entertaining, the preparation and the learning were all integrated into Mert's and my life there. In addition, though, all year long Sheldon Jackson College had on its staff and faculty many "Volunteers-in-Mission (VIM), and volunteers from churches came in the summer, too. In 1976, there was an especially large group: the grand "Yellow Banana" – a Hughes Airways plane - was chartered by 79 volunteers from Presbyterian Churches of Phoenix, Tempe, and Mesa, Arizona, who came to work at the college for two weeks! A few months later Mert and I were guests at a salmon bake fundraiser in Phoenix for SJC.

Such travel became a part of our lives. Periodically, Mert had to attend meetings of the Presbyterian Mission Schools which I could attend and I always learned a lot. We had opportunities to visit interesting sights in Alaska, too. Many times we were in Juneau, the capital for official college business. It was always special to worship in the Presbyterian Church there with the sanctuary facing Mendenhall Glacier.

Also, we were grateful for many family visits during our three years in Sitka – to see how we could live in Alaska. One visit included Mert's 90 year-old mother from Michigan.

When our three-year stint in SJC was coming to an end, I wrote Dr. Bratten at Lakeland Village. He replied immediately that the Title I program had been taken over by the Medical Lake School District and had become a part of its program at Lakeland Village School (LVS) on the institution's campus. Soon thereafter, I had a letter from Ted Salmon, Principal, offering me a teaching job.

Mert retired from Sheldon Jackson College in July 1977. Our years in Sitka were busy and exciting. We were happy to serve SJC but he was looking forward to his second and final retirement. I was looking forward to returning to Lakeland Village.

We flew back to Seattle, picked up our car, and drove to Spokane. In September, I joined the Medical Lake School District at Lakeland Village School as a special education teacher.

CHAPTER 10

"We glide along the tides of time as swiftly as a racing river, and vanish as quickly as a dream. We are like grass that is green in the morning but mowed down and withered before the evening shadows fall." (Psalm 90:5-6TLB)

WINTER SEASON ENDED IN THE SPRINGTIME

I had a few hours to reflect during our flight back to Seattle. I had a great opportunity to learn different cultures – Eskimos, Native Americans, and Japanese. I crossed cultural barriers by being immersed in who they are and how they live. From the Eskimos, I had learned that when hunting and fishing season began, hunting and fishing - their means of livelihood - had a higher priority than attending school. So, their English proficiency level and math skills were not where they should be for first year college students. I understood why Glen from Point Barrow had to sell me a whale baleen so he could go with his class to Spain. The baleen stills hangs in my home today. From the Native Americans, I learned the true value of taking from nature – fish, wild game, fowl – only what one needs. From the Japanese, I learned the value of time, and that it must be used productively. I had been able to build bridges between these groups and Sheldon Jackson College.

I felt a sense of contentment, yet a sense of trepidation surfaced when I thought of what was to come next. I had been fully cognizant of the wide disparity in our ages and professional attainment – Mert was in his winter season, whereas it was only my early summer. His retirement from Sheldon Jackson College at 70 was his second and he would be fully retired, whereas at almost 40 years old, I would be continuing from where I left off at Lakeland Village and could work for twenty or more years. Yet, I had made myself available to serve and wherever I would be and whatever I could do, I would give my best. I was grateful that a teaching job was waiting for me at Lakeland Village.

While I was in Alaska, it became mandatory that public schools admit "non-educable and "non-trainable children" into the school system. Upon returning, I joined Medical Lake District as a special education teacher on Lakeland campus. The School Board required in-district residence, so we sold our home in Spokane and had a home built on Silver Lake. It was designed by our friend and architect Taylor Potter and my only request was that I would have "picture windows," as the house would sit right on the lake. We moved into our new home in May 1978 and it proved to be the best for both of us. Mert loved fishing, gardening and landscaping and for me, it was only six-mile drive to Lakeland Village. Perfect! We resumed our active participation in church activities and invited the seniors group annually for a summer picnic at our place on the lake. Over the years the lake home had been filled with many wonderful memories of close friends and my nephews and niece growing up.

Ted Salmon, the Lakeland Village principal, was glad to have me "on board" because   he had heard so much of what I had done for children with severe and profound disabilities. He explained that my class load of 22 children included the most handicapped – deaf, blind, non-verbal and non-ambulatory. Our classrooms were in three different living units, but I had six very capable, efficient and loving teacher's aides.

By the time I went back to Lakeland, colleges and universities had come up with classes in special education. The

Psychology Department at Lakeland had refined our curriculum in the "Lakeland Village Adaptive Behavior Grid." This was a tremendous help. The "Grid" gave our work focus and allowed us to answer the question, "What exactly do we teach these children and how?" In the next few years, we would become more and more skillful in thinking about and realizing our goals for these children.

Within a few years the school-age population at Lakeland was dwindling. So in 1985, the school on campus was closed and the remaining 25 children were transported daily on a school bus to Blair Elementary School at Fairchild Air Force Base. Four teachers continued the Lakeland Village training and education program and I served as Coordinator.

By that time, we had Zack, a fifteen year-old, whose main problem was behavior. He would just leave class. One time he took off from the building but we were not concerned because we were inside the Base and he could go anywhere. The secretary had seen him leave and merely observed Zack. When he stopped at one place, she would call Base Security to say that I would be driving there to pick him up. Zack was surprised to see the car stopped next to him. I opened the door and told him to get in and he said, "Mrs. Munn, quick, the security will see us!"

We used Zack's ability to communicate to his advantage. Once, I talked about Native American fry bread and his eyes went big! He was a Native American. He asked, "Can we make fry bread?"

"Yes, once you learn to read the recipe correctly."

The home living teacher accommodated Zack's wish and it triggered a love for reading. Because it was so exciting to him, we told him that he could make fry bread and have it once a month. He really began to "buckle down" and work in school.

Someone asked where I got ideas to manage the behavior and teach students, like Zack. In those days, there was no Internet for doing research. I depended on books; education magazines; journals; special education workshops; conferences; conversations with other teachers I met and on observing the children's behavior inside and outside the classroom.

BLAIR ELEMENTARY SCHOOL

In February 1987, there was a major change in my career. The principal of Blair Elementary School had a fatal heart attack, and Duane Heidenreich, Medical Lake School District Superintendent, called to say that he needed me to be the replacement. The appointment was based on my performance as a teacher, an administrator – intermittent assistant principal at Lakeland Village, a coordinator and on active participation in School District activities. It was a shock, but there I was again: to fill in where I was needed. Duane introduced me at a faculty meeting and told them that I would be the principal for the remainder of the year. In the office, I asked Duane where to start.

He said, "Start from the top of the pile and find it out yourself. The only thing I need to say is you will be working with Base officials." I soon found out that meant the "Office of the Deputy Base Commander."

I called Mert to schedule a dinner at our regular place – Inn at the Park. Surprised, he said, "This is not Thursday; why?" Thursday evening was our regular dining out.

All I said was, "You are dining with an elementary school principal tonight." He could not believe it! He was so happy!

Blair Elementary School on Fairchild Air Force had 750 students and a contingent of 70 plus teachers and staff. The administrative staff – Assistant Principal, Curriculum Coordinator, and Food Services Manager all initiated me to the sudden responsibility and in the ensuing weeks and months, all the teachers and staff helped tremendously. It also required long hours of classroom observations and teacher evaluations but working with children directly or indirectly gave me a lot of pleasure.

That spring, I got to know many of the principals in the area. One of them warned me, "Femme, we are in line to apply for that principal's position at Blair when it is announced." I said, "Fine." However, at the end of that school year, Duane said, "Femme, you can have your job for as long as you want it." "The Lord is my Pilot and the Bible is my compass."

I had been prepared for this work by my education and by my administrative experience at Lakeland, and I gained more knowledge working with superintendents, administrative colleagues, teachers and staff who worked with me during my six and a half years I was at Blair. Together, we made Blair Elementary School lived up to its motto, "A Great Place to Be."

Then, because of my years of experience in special education and being principal of an elementary school, I was invited in the spring of 1988 to conduct a workshop on special education for the public school teachers and government officials in Pago Pago, American Samoa. The invitation was made through Mert's daughter, Gwen Long who was a reading specialist in Pago

Pago. I used the Lakeland Village Adaptive Behavior Grid and walked the participants through assessment of children with disabilities, curriculum, and training methods.

It was a great experience to meet Samoans – a very friendly people. I spent an afternoon with third graders in one of the schools. Mert and I attended functions in many schools and quite often returned loaded with food. Both boys and girls dressed in "wrap around" skirts and in all schools we visited, dances were performed by students in colorful costumes. On the flight back to Spokane, I reflected on American Samoan schools, how isolated they were and how much need there was in all the buildings. Even their school libraries needed upgrading, yet they are a happy people. I shared this experience with teachers and staff at Blair.

The highlight of my experience at Blair Elementary School and of my association with Fairchild Air Force Base personnel was the visit of Washington State Governor Booth Gardner on February 28, 1991. We had programs and an elegant reception planned but what made the day very special was that "Desert Storm" – the Gulf War- ended! Jubilation and celebration burst out everywhere. The Air Force Brass from Fairchild and the Governor and his entourage filled our school gym. What an honor and a privilege to sit on stage with these people to deliver my speech. I was in high spirits!

Throughout the years that I was Principal, Mert went with me to all the conference I attended, including two conventions. This included two conventions of National Elementary School Principals –in San Antonio, Texas in 1990 and in San Francisco in 1992. In San Francisco, 26,000 elementary school principals gathered. I was one of the Washington State delegates to the

National Assembly of 400. Mert sat proudly in the gallery watching the proceedings on the floor. It was through him that I had attained this level in my career. He knew that I was enjoying my work very much and he was enjoying being retired on Silver Lake.

THE END OF WINTER SEASON

When I was hired permanent principal of Blair Elementary School, Duane asked how many years I would be able to serve. I told him anywhere from three to five years depending on my husband's health. I was there almost seven years.

Mert expressed many times how happy he was of my accomplishment in my profession, but he was proud also of the educational attainment of members of my family. We had sponsored my younger siblings Rachel and Ben and their spouses for advanced studies at Oregon State University. Rachel and Laraine attained their Master's Degrees. Gideon and Ben both eventually got their PhD. Ben is my only sibling to attain a Doctorate Degree. At the same time we assisted many in the Philippines to get their college education. He was constantly amazed at my large family. He jokingly said that children of the younger generation would likely fill up a school, so we should build and develop one in Balabagan.

In my sixth year as Principal, Mert's health started to decline. In June 1993, I took an early retirement. The decision was a big surprise to him, knowing how much I enjoyed my work. I told him that he was my top priority. Fortunately for me, it just happened that in the spring of 1993, the Washington State Legislature had passed a bill that anyone could retire at age 55 regardless of years of service. I had turned 55 and, yes, I could retire with full benefits. So I did.

Early retirement was a wise decision. I spent quality time with Mert and we travelled, mostly to Corvallis or the Oregon Coast. He had always wanted to see Bryce Canyon, so Rachel and Gideon arranged a special trip in the spring of 1994. Mert could not take his eyes off the snow-covered Wasatch Mountains en route and fully embraced the magnificence of Bryce Canyon. His health continued to decline and exactly a year later, on March 20, 1995, he crossed the threshold into the next life. It happened in the springtime.

Standing L-R: Rachel, Josephine, Jovencia, Virgilio, Josue, Jeremias, Constancio, Remedios, Fely, Eufemia Sitting: Cayetano and Gabriela (Parents) Forefront: Abraham and Benjamin

Blair Elementary School Staff Photo Author is Front row 5th from the Left

Guo Family: Sitting L-R - Kevin, M/M George Guo, Eufemia Munn Standing: Gary, Wendy, Tim Guo

Eufemia Munn in Lanao del Sur Mindanao Philippines

L-R: Pastor Dan Tobias, Ms. Purita Bahande, Josephine Rivera, Mayor Edna Benito Ugka, Friend, Rev. Lumapguid, Bishop H. Gomez, Virgilio Tobias

Fw: L-R: Remedios Samonte, Josephine Rivera, Dr. Ben Tobias, Hildo Rivera, "INA" Ponsing Ugka, Jovencia Hofer

Dr. Andrew Tsoi, Eufemia Munn - Qufu, China

Qingdao International School, China: Lisa Zhang (TA) and 5th Grade Students

Great Wall China: Jessica, Kevin, Fei Fei

Amanda & John's Wedding

Eufemia Munn In Chile

Eufemia Munn on Easter Island (Rapa Nui)

Tobias-Munn Wedding: Mrs. Maria Clara Lobregat, Vicente Hofer, Sponsors: Fred Appleton, Best Man; Rachel Tobias, Bridesmaid

Silliman University Gates Dumaguete City, Neros Oriental, Phipippines

Shalom Science Institute First High School Classroom

CHAPTER 11

"Oh for wings like a dove to fly away and rest,
I would fly to the far off desert and stay there.
I would flee to some refuge from the storms"
(Psalm 55:6-7 TLB)

A TURNING POINT

An amazing active life ground to a halt when Mert passed on in the spring of 1995. Half of me died with him but I had to force myself to take care of paper work and numerous tasks following his death. I turned inward. All I wanted was to be alone with my thoughts. I lived in the past. I read all his letters again and again while making frequent visits to the cemetery. I made a scrapbook of his memorial service and worked on photo albums. I wrote letters to him in my journals. Except for Church and Presbytery committee meetings, I stayed away from anything that distracted me from thinking of my past life. I quit entertaining or even cooking for myself. I became a recluse on Silver Lake.

Mert's estate took nine months to settle, and when it was finished in January 1996, I felt liberated. That fall, I made a few trips to visit Rachel and Gideon in Corvallis. Their family and my nephew, Chris at Whitworth College had been very supportive throughout my grieving. My family from Australia - Chris' parents and his brother, Julius from Melbourne and Bing Rivera, my niece, from Perth visited that winter. My niece, Ana Fe, and her family came from San Francisco to celebrate Christmas with us. It was the beginning of my coming into life again.

That January 1996, Julius remained and lived with me to attend Medical Lake High School. His presence gave me the incentive to prepare meals again and I gradually went to school events, this time as a "parent." I transported him to school daily and when he came home from school, he enjoyed a bowl of rice smothered with thick chili. Then he did his homework before dinner. He spent his weekends with Chris at Whitworth but on Sundays, the three of us met and attended Whitworth Community Presbyterian Church.

I used to tell people that a job is good therapy. I did not have a job. I took an early retirement. I had to confront the question, "What now and where?" I was aware of the fact that Julius would be with me for a few years. Then, a year after Mert died, I decided to live again! I can't explain why or how I broke out of this "funk." It was more a combination of family and sense of duty to others that I felt the need to rejoin society. I was still young and had so much more to give! In the spring of 1996, I spent hours in the yard and garden. I browsed and studied magazines about plants. Mert was the gardener and now it had fallen on me to do the work. I took piano lessons, joined the P.E.O and I joined AMWAY through Chris, who had joined the business and was getting very involved.

THE AMWAY BUSINESS

I was intrigued by the AMWAY business concept. It required hard work as any business does, but I enjoyed getting to meet and to know people. The products were excellent and I sold a lot. I did one-on-one presentations, I attended home meetings and I went to conventions near and far. In 1997, I went with the Spokane contingent to the AMWAY opening in the Philippines. I held my own meetings in Mindanao - Davao, Balabagan, Cagayan de Oro and in Negros Oriental - Siaton and Dumaguete City. I attended other meetings, usually in large hotel auditorium planned by AMWAY management and Worldwide Dream Builders.

That trip was a way to find out if it was really what I wanted to do in retirement from public school.

While waiting for my flight in Manila airport to the opening meetings in Cebu City, I talked to a woman whose niece desperately needed heart surgery. I arranged to meet three year-old Desiree Potot between meetings at Midtown Hotel in Cebu. I was touched and I offered to submit her medical evaluations to "Healing the Children, Spokane Chapter (HTC)." It was not long before Desiree's case was approved. She came to live with Jim and Shirl Lewis, foster parents, while waiting for her heart surgery and while in recovery. Desiree finally had her surgery at Deaconess Hospital in 1998. At that time, I also submitted Charisma Sansolis' medical evaluations. Her case was similar and she was from my hometown, Balabagan. HTC also accepted her case and she came in February 2000. Like Desiree, she also stayed with Jim and Shirl. Charisma had her surgery at Sacred Heart Medical Center. Desiree and Charisma are alive today and pursuing college education because of my AMWAY connection.

The social part of AMWAY was always fun. I met new people, but travel involved risks. On October 28, 1998 I was on my way to a one-on-one AMWAY meeting when I had a major accident in Airway Heights. Except for skin abrasions on my shoulder from seatbelt, I was not harmed and the other driver stayed in the hospital only overnight. However, it took three months to repair my brand new Dodge Caravan.

Then, two weeks after I got the van back, I hit black ice on the bend at the east end of the causeway near my home. Again, I was not injured, but the vehicle went back for more repairs. Were these signs that I needed to move on? Through that winter and spring, I was beginning to realize that doing the AMWAY business was difficult without transportation. Also, my nephew Chris had gotten married and moved to San Jose to begin his new life. So, without transportation and my AMWAY personal support system, I gradually eased out of the business.

I continued with piano lessons and in addition to PEO, I also attended meetings of Phi Lamba Theta and the American Association of University Women. My older sister, Remy, visited her daughter in California for a year and came to visit me a number of times. I had not been with Remy for more than four decades, so it was very special that we could spend time together. Growing up she was always the kindest sister to me. She would help me in the fields when harvesting corn and with my chores at home. Now, I had great pleasure from watching her experience new things here, like fishing off the dock for hours, watching her favorite show, "The Price is Right" and taking her on driving trips.

Julius spent that summer with his parents, who had come from Australia for the wedding of his brother, Chris. I had healed from grieving considerably and was considering my future. When Julius returned for his senior year, I started applying for overseas employment with the Department of Defense Dependent Schools (DODDS) and the U.S. Air Force. I was offered one in Ramstein, Germany, but Julius was still with me.

Then, three years after the Airway Heights accident, I was confronted with a lawsuit from the other driver. The telephone woke me up from an afternoon nap. My Farmer's Insurance agent said, "You better get a lawyer. The party refuses our settlement because you are a widow and may have inherited a lot of money. They have also found out that you have a lake home."

"How soon do you want the lawyer?" I said.

"Work on it now. I want to talk to him tomorrow," he replied.

I was stunned! I had been able to navigate through the death of my husband and many financial decisions but how could I get through this? I remembered the law firm in Spokane where Mert's friend, Glover Patterson, had been our lawyer. Although Glover had passed away the previous year, I went to the law office. The secretary said, "Oh, we have a lawyer who specializes in vehicular accidents." She rang and Richard Lewis, a young gentleman came out to meet me. His warm voice put me at ease. He remembered us as clients of the firm and I told him about my case.

He listened to all the details about the accident and asked a lot of questions. I told him that once the case was settled I would get away. Perhaps I could go to Savoonga on St. Laurence Island in the Bering Sea to teach.

"You need not go that far," he said. "We have a school in Alaska, you can teach there."

"Who is 'we' and where is the school?" I asked,

"Oh, it is Sheldon Jackson College in Sitka, Alaska."

For a moment, I stepped back in time. I looked at him and said,

"My late husband, Dr. Merton Munn was president of Sheldon Jackson College."

"Oh yes, I recall his wife was Chinese." He said.

"Well, I am the wife. I am not Chinese. I am Filipino," I replied. "Are you Presbyterian?" I asked.

"Oh yes, my family and I attend First Presbyterian Church in Spokane." Then he said, "Don't agonize over this. We will take care of you."

What a relief! He took the case. I was on pins and needles while waiting for the result of the lawsuit. Two months later, a settlement was reached and the lawsuit was dropped!

Relieved, the following day I took a long drive to Trail, British Columbia and had lunch there. I drove west to another Border Gate to re-enter the U.S.A. and drove along the Columbia River to Grand Coulee Dam then to Davenport and home to Medical Lake. The long daytrip eased the burden and cleared my mind.

There had been a series of negative events in my recent life but the lawsuit seemed to bring a turning point. It definitely appeared that I shouldn't be in Medical Lake. Where could I again find a life with purpose and joy? If not DODDS or the U.S. Air Force, where? How could I press ahead? I decided to go home to the Philippines. "The Lord is my Pilot and the Bible is my Compass."

CHAPTER 12

"Oh that you would wonderfully bless me and help me in my work;
please be with me in all that I do,
and keep me from all evil and disaster"
(1Chronicles 4:10 TLB)

"WAR ON MUSLIM REBELS"

My vision for my life was obscured by my husband's death, ensuing challenges, vehicular accidents, and a lawsuit. I had to stand still and listen. Only then could I discern what I was destined to do next. Positive events began to help me find the way.

Mert and had joined Whitworth Community Presbyterian Church in Spokane and through the years, I had served as deacon, elder and representative to the Presbytery. In June 1997, I had been elder commissioner to the Presbyterian Church (USA) General Assembly in Syracuse, New York. There, up in the gallery was Dr. Jan Beran, a missionary at Silliman University. I saw her after one of the sessions and we had a good visit. She and I attended a dinner for the Young Adult Volunteers (YAV), who had been appointed to serve in the Philippines. I also visited with Patricia Mack Churchman, daughter of Dr. Henry and Margaret Mack, who were also missionaries at Silliman. These events took my mind back to my home country.

When Julius graduated in June 2000, I decided to go to the Philippines. I was not afraid of going home to Balabagan despite news of rampant danger due to Muslim rebels. Because of that courage, I asked myself, "Is that where I am destined to serve?"

THE FALL OF CAMP ABUBAKAR

In July 2000, Philippine President Joseph Estrada declared "War on Muslim Rebels." That summer was the height of radical Muslim rebel infiltration in the provinces of Lanao del Sur and Maguindanao. The Moro Islamic Liberation Front (MILF) had gradually taken control of an enclave of 10,000 square kilometers, including Balabagan and in the process, had displaced hundreds of families – Christians and Muslims. The MILF had its headquarters at Camp Abubakar in Matanog at the boundary between the provinces of Lanao del Sur and Maguindanao on the Narciso Ramos Highway. My oldest brother, Virgilio who also possessed the calmest disposition, worked with the Bureau of Lands and had visited Camp Abubakar when it was in full operation by the rebels. He said that it had become a sprawling self-contained village with a hospital, merchandise store, mosque, homes and the Abdulrhaman Bedis Memorial Academy.

There had been skirmishes between government troops and rebels before but then there was an ambush of government trucks and soldiers were killed. A raid by a band of armed men suspected to be MILF rebels massacred twenty residents in a village in Bumbaran, Lanao del Sur. These incidents and other attacks precipitated the bombing of Camp Abubakar.

It was under these dangerous conditions that I had decided to visit my hometown. The Narciso Ramos Highway between Cotabato City and Lanao del Sur was closed because of the fighting. When I arrived in Manila, my flight to Cotabato Airport had to be changed to Dumaguete City. My brother, Dr. Benjamin Tobias, Dean of Silliman University College of Engineering, met me in Manila and we flew to Dumaguete City

From Dumaguete, Ben and I took the Supercraft boat to Dapitan, Zamboanga del Norte where we took a bus and arrived in Oroquieta, Misamis Occidental in time for lunch. We bought boiled bananas and boiled eggs "for the road" and our bus continued on to Ozamiz City, where we took a ferry across to Tubod in Lanao del Norte. I enjoyed the trip until we reached Marawi City.

Marawi is the Muslim capital of the Philippines with 90% Muslim population. Aida Tobias Lendio, my niece, met us in Marawi Lanao del Sur. A 1977 graduate of Silliman University, Aida is the Municipal Agriculturist of Balabagan and her job requires many trips to Marawi. As agriculturist, she serves both Christians and Muslims. Her work area includes barrios along Narciso Ramos Highway but she had also cultivated very good relationships with Muslims beyond the boundary, including the area near Matanog, where Camp Abubakar is located. Similarly, Edwina, Aida's sister, is Assistant to the Muslim mayor of Kapatagan, near Abubakar. Like their father, Virgilio, Aida and Edwina both reached out to the Muslims and had gained their respect.

From Marawi, we rode with Aida in a van to Malabang. When I took a seat away from a window, Aida handed me a scarf (kumbong) and said,

"Cover your head with this and keep quiet."

I sat quietly in the van. I began to realize that I was a "foreigner." Later, I learned that many questioned my sanity in putting me in harm's way, but I did not feel any fear at all.

Soon after I arrived in Balabagan, I persuaded my siblings to take me to Barangay Itil, my birthplace. Virgilio, who was a

Balabagan Councilor in the 1980's, had to consult Edna Benito Ugka, Mayor of Balabagan, for security. She is a Muslim with a degree in dentistry. She gave us clearance but insisted that we use her van and her driver. It was a bumpy ride on an unpaved road for six kilometers to the highway but it did not bother me at all. Sights along the way rekindled memories of my childhood and youth. It was my first visit since I left our homestead decades ago.

Itil Elementary School had become a military compound and the schoolyard was filled with military trucks and armed personnel. Cannons were lined up on the grounds. Virgilio recognized the Colonel, the head of the military detachment. With a concerned look in his eyes, the Colonel asked me,

"Why are you here? This is a dangerous place right now," he said.

"I was born here," I replied. "I wanted to see this place again. In fact, two hectares of our homestead were donated by my parents for this public school." I asked,

"May I take pictures of those cannons over there?

"Take pictures, but do not touch them. Those are still hot; they were just fired to Camp Abubakar," he said.

We shook hands with the Colonel and expressed our gratitude. Just then, Mayor Edna appeared and escorted us back to Balabagan.

The cannons were still hot from having been fired when my siblings and I visited Barangay Itil because our visit was just several hours after Camp Abubakar fell to the Philippine military on July 9, 2000. And soon thereafter, a training camp of Jimaah Islamiyah, a few kilometers from Balabagan, moved out.

Actually, Mayor Edna is my niece, in the Filipino way of thinking. She is the granddaughter of Sultan Sampiano of Barorao who had protected our family in his Sultanate during World War II. One of the Sultan's sons, Ugka, married Ponsing, my mother's cousin (Edna's mother) during the War. The family had extended kindness and hospitality to Christians and these traits of the family endeared them to my relatives. So when she fell in love with Ugka, it was okay for her to marry into the Sampiano family. She embraced their Muslim faith and through the years, through her, a bridge had been built between her Muslim family and us, her Christian family. "Ina," (mother) as we fondly call Ponsing, is clear manifestation of the idea that differences in culture and faith can merge together with respect and understanding. Edna considers my siblings and me as her "aunts" and "uncles." So we, in return, consider her our "niece." Mayor Edna's role in Balabagan at the height of in-fighting between two Muslim factions and the rebels against the government was precarious at best, but she performed her duties as Government Official very well.

When we visited Barangay Itil, for some reason, I felt no fear at all. However, my sisters said, it was good that I did not look like a tourist. My camera was in a plastic bag; I wore a scarf, no make-up and no lipstick. When we got home, my family sat me down and gave me an intense briefing on Camp Abubakar. Then, I became aware of the very extreme danger that they were living with.

In the ensuing months, relative peace and security were restored. Narciso Ramos Highway again became passable with military checkpoints along the way, but travel still was dangerous and people were advised to do it only during daytime.

In no time, the whole community knew about my presence in Balabagan. My family could only assure my safety by exercising extreme caution. My problem was that I liked to go around, especially to visit the public market to see and talk to vendors which I did almost daily. Oh, I loved the abundance of fresh seafood! Of course, it also helped that I can speak the local Muslim dialect – Maranao.

The caution that I exercised strictly was not to go out at night. By sundown, I was inside the house. It was not unusual to hear surveillance helicopters. One day, a nephew said, "Yesterday, when we were at the beach for the picnic, did you notice those men in civilian clothes in the shed near us?"

"Yes, I did. Why?" I replied.

"Well, they seemed to be having a picnic also, but really, they were your security. They were there as part of military surveillance whenever you are in the area."

"Oh, is that right? I had no idea." Just then, I truly felt the gravity of the situation for me personally and from then on, I was much more careful.

The rebel infiltration had uprooted families – Christians and Muslims – from their farms and homes. A good many sought refuge in Balabagan. The town was filled with refugees who had put up makeshift shelters. Fearful of retaliation from rebels, refugees would not return to their farms, and their children's education was drastically disrupted. The local public school had opened its doors to these refugee children but every classroom was soon severely overcrowded. I took a tour and visited some classrooms. They were so overcrowded that I couldn't see how learning was possible. My heart ached for those children.

I began to think in earnest about Shalom Learning School still in an early stage of development with only kindergarten to second grade. Could I serve here or should I return to the U.S.A and find something else. Shalom was well-managed but the Department of Education (DepEd) required an administrator with a master's degree. To understand better, I accompanied Aida Lendio to the DepEd office in Cotabato City to present the school's application for a permit. It was clear that a permit would be contingent upon having a qualified administrator and the fulfillment of a few other requirements. On the way home, Aida persuaded me to help them. The Board already had a strategic plan to develop by adding a grade a year. Of course, I said, "YES."

I went to work! I reviewed documents; visited classrooms; met with teachers, staff and the School Board. Goals and objectives had already been drawn up; they highlighted how to build the bridge across cultural and religious differences. One major objective was to offer quality education to both Christians and Muslims and through it, cultivate positive relationships with all the parents and others in the community.

I accepted the challenge to help build and develop Shalom Learning School as a "volunteer administrator." I felt strongly that it was at Shalom where I was needed. In1992 during a visit in Balabagan, Mert had predicted - "Someday, you will be back to serve your people."

When I made that decision to serve Shalom Learning School, it was in July 2000, right on the heels of "War on Muslim Rebels," but I felt the courage and the confidence that I was needed and would be safe.

I left Balabagan, promising to return in a few months. I flew to Dumaguete City to fulfill commitments at Silliman University and then returned to the U.S.A.

CHAPTER 13

"What do you have there in your hand? -----
------a shepherd's rod" (Exodus 4:2 TLB)

SHALOM SCIENCE INSTITUTE

At the time this book is being written (2013), Shalom Learning School had become Shalom Science Institute, Incorporated (SSI) after high school classes were added in June 2010. The school went through reorganization and a month later, it was officially registered with the Securities and Exchange Commission. My brother, Dr. Benjamin Tobias, who was instrumental in making this change was the original President of SSI. Shalom Science Institute Foundation was also organized with Arnel Hofer as President. SSI's first high school graduation will be in March 2014.

Shalom was a fledgling non-profit Christian school when I made a commitment to serve. I left Balabagan that summer of 2000, wondering: Where would I begin? How would I begin? These were my questions during my two-week stay at Silliman University.

Ben met me at Dumaguete Airport. He drove to the campus, unloaded my luggage in his apartment and whisked me off to Malatapay Resort, about 20 kilometers south of Dumaguete. It was a perfect afternoon for coffee and my favorite - pan de sal (bread rolls). He briefed me on my schedule of activities and we talked. The relaxing atmosphere of Malatapay was just what I needed! I soaked in the sea with Apo Island in the distance and savored the warm breeze. A dry crescent moon graced the sky when we finished dinner.

The first event on my schedule was a speech at a Silliman University College of Engineering Convocation. Held in Silliman Church, there were 1,000 students. Actually, I found answers to my questions where and how to begin my work in Balabagan, right in the text of my own speech, "What Is It in Your Hands?" I pressed students, first, to discover what they had been equipped with and second, to use it. Was it a coincidence that I chose that topic when I prepared my talk for this convocation? What I shared with students also spoke deeply to my own heart. It opened a way for me to assess my own capabilities and abilities - to help build and develop Shalom Learning School.

Ben and I planned to publish "A Quest for Excellence in Christian Higher Education" by Dr. Merton Munn, not only as a tribute to Mert but also as part of the Silliman University Centennial Celebration. It was a compilation of articles that he had written for Silliman University Journals.

I had written Dr. Cicero Calderon, former president of Silliman University and asked him to write the "Foreword" to the book. So I had asked Ben to put on my schedule a lunch meeting with Dr. Calderon. When I arrived in Dumaguete, Ben told me that Dr. Calderon insisted that we had dinner with him in his residence. Dr. Edith Tiempo, a retired Silliman University professor and National Artist for Literature, was there. The following week, we had dinner with her in Montemar – her home overlooking the ocean. Dr. Calderon was there, too. Both of them had ideas that inspired my plans for Shalom.

Next, Ben and I hosted a dinner party at Bethel Guest House for our Silliman University friends and colleagues and for the College of Engineering faculty and staff. What a pleasure it was to see so many attended! I informed them that Mert's book would be published for the Silliman Centennial Celebration in 2001.

Those two weeks in Dumaguete helped me sort out the challenges ahead. The long flight back to Seattle and Spokane gave me time to gather my thoughts about my work for Shalom. During the ensuing months, I raised funds for classrooms, collected and shipped books and pondered: How a tiny Christian school in a remote and impoverished area, right in the heart of the ARMM (Autonomous Region of Muslim Mindanao) could be developed to have an impact on a community of 60% Christians and 40% Muslims? More simply, how could a Christian school bridge the gap between Christians and Muslims? After all, they are Filipinos, too.

A SEED PLANTED WHERE COCONUTS GROW

How did Shalom Learning School begin? The idea came from Mert to members of the Balabagan United Church of Christ. During our intermittent visits to the Philippines, he usually could not go with me to Balabagan for security reasons. Rebels had infiltrated the area since our wedding, years before. Two Muslim groups were fighting each other and skirmishes were on the rise. He had always wished to visit the place again, so in July 1992, we took a chance while we were on a "Circle Pacific Tour," courtesy of a very generous benefactor. For security, we had to charter a small plane for the twelve-minute flight from Cotabato City to the airstrip at the Balabagan Coconut Estate (BCE). We stayed in the Lobregat home. There was a military detachment in Balabagan

111

and everyone took extreme caution because anyone could be caught in the crossfire. I thought our visit in Balabagan would be kept quiet but our family had planned a reunion in the BCE guest house - brand new at the time of our wedding twenty six years before.

The United Church of Christ is downtown and travel to the worship service at which Mert was the speaker had to be timed when there was a lull in the fighting. Look-outs were sent to different areas to assure security while we were at the church. After the worship service, we walked around the Church property and came upon a small one-room building with thatch roof, cement floor and knee-high hollow blocks. A church elder said, "It is too bad we use it only for Sunday school."

Without blinking an eye, Mert said, "Why don't you use it for preschool during the week?" He had planted the seed for the school!

I thought the congregation would be more discreet about our visit but in front of the church building was a huge banner, "Welcome Dr. and Mrs. Munn!" In retrospect, it was just as well that the banner was up there to announce to the Muslims that there were "outsiders" who dared to tread on dangerous grounds. There was a lull in the fighting. We would have loved to have gone to the beach but security was precarious at best. The military was there but we had to be cautious.

A week later, the charter plane came to pick us up for the return trip to Cotabato City. Waving to people at the airstrip, Mert said to me, "Someday, you will come home and serve your people."

"Serve my people in what way?" I asked. He looked at me and said, "Just make yourself open to God's plan. When the right time comes, you will know."

I thought nothing more of what he had said.

LITTLE FOOTSTEPS, SMALL VOICES

Rev. Nathan Roa was pastor of Balabagan United Church of Christ when Mert and I visited in 1992. Shortly thereafter, he married Flordeliz, also a Silliman University graduate. She had a degree in early childhood education and in July 1995 four months after Mert died, she started the preschool program. The seed was beginning to grow.

When I visited in July 1997, I saw Shalom Learning School with 22 preschoolers. There were the sounds of small voices and little footsteps. Parents – Christians and Muslims – were asking for a kindergarten and higher grades so that their children could continue in the school's program. In July 2000, when I decided to help develop the school, it already had Kindergarten to Grade 2, and the School Board had in place a strategic plan to add a grade a year.

In March 2001, I returned to Balabagan as a volunteer school administrator. My first priority was to start the library, but where? There was no spare space anywhere at the school. I asked my brother, Virgilio, if I could utilize his living room for the school library. He lived alone by then and his residence across the street from Shalom was fairly large. He said, "Yes, of course but there are no tables or chairs."

"That is not a problem. We have books and those are the most important for a library." Then I asked, "Who among our family is building a house?"

Our niece Redempta and her husband, Arnel, were building a house. I borrowed hollow blocks and planks from them. Those who were with me were fascinated at what I was doing. I really had lots of fun setting hollow blocks against the wall and laying the planks on them for book shelves. We would just spread out woven mats on the cool cement floor for reading groups. Who would help me sort out and catalog those books? What did I know about library work? I had never been a librarian! However, before I left for the Philippines, I had a one-hour crash course from our librarian at Whitworth Community Presbyterian Church library. With ideas that she taught me, I trained my family – two nieces and my sister, Josephine who had just retired from government service. We worked hard and got the project done before the end of the school year and we managed to have each grade come to the library at least once to meet their new "friends" – books!

I adjusted well to a life in a rural town and enjoyed my family very much. I also loved the abundance of seafood and fruit. However, it was an eye opener to see the living conditions of many people – displaced from their farms and seeking safety from radical Muslim rebels. Many had chosen to remain in Balabagan even after Camp Abubakar fell.

Shalom Learning School was becoming a good alternative to the overcrowded public schools due to the influx of refugee children. It followed DepEd curriculum and core values were being taught. Muslim parents were made aware and had accepted that the class day would begin with a prayer. I observed in the

114

classroom how this was done. The teacher would say, "Let us pray." Christian children would bow their heads with folded hands and Muslim children would extend their arms out with open hands. Together, they were praying but each according to their family's tradition.

It did not take long for me to discover that money was the primary issue. The school had been limping along financially with resources generated only from tuition and donations. One morning, with roosters crowing, a knock on my door woke me up. It was my niece, Redempta, who said, "I am sorry to bother you, but I don't have enough money to pay teachers and staff."

I grabbed my purse and counted whatever I had in it. She and I went to the kitchen for coffee and discussed school finance. The money I had raised and brought from the United States was barely enough to change a building's thatch roof into a tin roof. There were absolutely no funds in sight for classrooms and future program development.

I soon met with the School Board and discussed all that I had seen, heard and done. It was apparent that I had to return to the United States to search for a source to fund development. We looked for my replacement immediately. Fortunately, a public school principal had just retired and agreed to help us out.

About that time, a group of Protestant Pastors and Catholic Clergy came to visit Mayor Edna of Balabagan for a possible dialogue between Christians and Muslims. I was invited to go with the group. Mayor Edna graciously listened to the group's proposal. Then - speaking interchangeably in Cebuano, English and Maranao – she forthrightly said, "Dialogue is good but it is only talking. What we want is for Christians to show us a better way, like Shalom Learning School. It offers very good education program for our children. That is why many Muslim children are enrolled in Shalom."

That was unexpected. Mayor Edna's words strengthened my conviction that thoughtfully planned education could help bridge cultural and religious barriers and promote understanding, peace, and harmony.

The school year ended, and on April 5, 2001, I boarded a United Airlines flight to Seattle. We had to continue to build the bridge, and we needed funds. I had to find an extra source. Where? The plane took off, leaving behind winking lights of Manila.

CHAPTER 14

"Tell me where you want me to go, and I will go there.
May every fiber of my being unite in reverence to your Name.
With all my heart I will praise You.
I will give glory to Your Name forever."
(Psalm 86: 11-12TLB)

FLIGHT INTO THE UNKNOWN

I flew back to Spokane determined to build and develop Shalom Learning School. I wondered who would hire a 63 year-old retired principal of an elementary school. I did not want to work in the USA again. I had declined an offer with the US Air Force to work in a child development center in Ramstein, Germany due to time a conflict. Yet, I was confident that somewhere my services were needed. Where? "The Lord is my Pilot and the Bible is my compass."

THOUSANDS OF MILES INTO CHINA

I arrived home on Sunday afternoon, picking up our local newspaper, the Spokesman Review (SR). As soon as I got settled, I looked at the SR classifieds. My eyes were grasped by an employment advertisement: "If you want to teach in China, call this number."

I called the number Monday morning and it was Dr. Larae Palmanter, Superintendent of Qingdao International School (QIS) in China. She was in Pullman, Washington, recruiting teachers. Our conversation turned out to be a semi-interview and when she invited me to see her in Pullman, I said, "I am 63 years old and retired,"

She replied, "Oh, but your voice is still strong. Come to China and help me."

I made an appointment to see her in Pullman. We would meet at a well-known restaurant.

It was a snowy mid-April day and I almost decided not to go. There was a freak late season snowstorm which would slow my drive to Pullman. However, I decided to go anyway. By the time I got half-way there the snow had stopped and the roads were clear.

So, in my black suit, white blouse, black pumps and a brief case, I walked into the restaurant with confidence. There she was, an attractive lady with large eyes and a broad smile in a Chinese mandarin jacket. Larae showed me photos of Qingdao International School and offered me a choice of three jobs: to teach English as a second language; to teach a self-contained classroom in QIS campus in Qingdao; or to be principal-teacher in a new school in Beijing. I took Beijing, which she had hoped would be my choice.

I told her that I would go to China with these thoughts: "I do not want to cook and I do not want to do house cleaning."

"Perfect," she said. "You will live in a school apartment with maid service and you will have your meals in the cafeteria." Then she asked, "Aren't you going to ask about salary?"

"Yes, of course! How much are you going to pay me?" I asked.

You will get an annual salary, free board, and an apartment on campus, shipping of personal belongings, health benefits and free airline ticket."

I was stunned! I told her that with that extra untaxed money, I could certainly help build and develop Shalom Learning School in my hometown in the Philippines.

She continued. "Qingdao International School is a private school. The owners are a Taiwanese-American family from Queens, New York. QIS operates on a curriculum based on the United States education system and it offers kindergarten to high school. Since you agree, a QIS contract and the necessary documents will be sent to you."

"Where is Qingdao?" I asked.

"Qingdao is located in Shandong province in East China." She replied.

I asked about school vacations. I told her that I would expect to return to the Philippines during those vacations to work at Shalom. (China's proximity to the Philippines enabled me to spend working vacations in Balabagan.)

This was simply amazing! It had only been nine days since I had arrived and I had gotten a teaching job -- China! I was overjoyed! I had to stop in a restaurant in Colfax to calm down from this fast turn of events. While I was eating, a lady who had been shooting glances at me, came over and said,

"I just cannot help it. I must tell you that you look so professional – seldom seen these days. Are you a teacher?"

"Yes, I am! In fact, I had just been hired to teach in China. I came to Pullman for an interview with the superintendent of an international school." I replied.

"Congratulations! I just came home from a wonderful tour of China and I would like to go again." she said, and added, "You will like it there."

HOPPING LIKE A TOAD ON A RAINY DAY

I called my sister Rachel and her husband in Corvallis, Oregon.   Rachel said, "What did you say? Packing for China? You've just arrived from the Philippines!"

"Yes, I will teach in China and school begins the last week of August." I said.

Then Gideon got on the phone. We discussed summer plans and events – their son's wedding, our trip for the Silliman University Centennial Celebration in Dumaguete City and family reunions.   I told him that I would fly to Beijing from the Philippines.

The next three months happened at a frenetic pace: packing, taking care of China documents, getting the house and garden in order. I felt a lot of stress but working in the garden, which was necessary too, was also releasing. With so much on my mind and my heart beating with excitement, I shoved the shovel deep into the ground and dug up weeds. I raked the lawn with all my might and planted Early Girl tomatoes. I would occasionally take a long walk along the lake to soak in the landscape and bring home the firm assurance that God is in control.

Then it was time to leave. Parting from my home again was difficult. With some regret and with some trepidation, I took

120

a last look at my house: flowers blooming, green tomatoes filling the vines, the lake twinkling and the locust trees profuse with white blossoms. I turned to leave - but I couldn't find the key to the van. It took an hour for a technician from the dealership to come with a replacement. An hour later in Perkins Restaurant in Ritzville, I took time to enjoy my breakfast: pancakes, eggs, bacon and a pot of coffee. I figured that I would not have such a breakfast in China.

My dear sister was almost fit to be tied because it was dark by the time I arrived in Corvallis. I told her about the lost key and we began unloading boxes and bags from the van. Then, I took out groceries from a brown bag because I had put a container of cooked trout fish in it. There was my van key at the bottom of the bag!

The few days in Corvallis were also busy. G-mer Alegado's wedding was on August 4, 2001. On August 6 I flew with Rachel, Gideon and Garnet, their daughter to Dumaguete City.

SILLIMAN UNIVERSITY CENTENNIAL CELEBRATION

Since my late husband, Dr. Merton Munn, had been a Presbyterian missionary at Silliman University for nearly nine years, we decided to honor him with four events at the Centennial celebration: Garnet gave a piano/organ recital in Silliman University Church; I reviewed his work at Silliman in a forum - "Excellence in Education," we launched his book – A Quest for Excellence in Christian Higher Education; and Ben and I hosted the "Munn Renaissance Banquet" attended by former missionaries, colleagues and thirty-four members of my own family.

In the midst of the many Centennial events, I was jolted with a cablegram from Cathy George, Principal of Qingdao International School in China. "Beijing school is not going to open. Come to Qingdao to teach Grade 5. Come as soon as you can."

I gave the cablegram to Rachel. With a concerned look, she asked, "Where is Qingdao? Your airline ticket is only to Beijing."

"Qingdao is in Shandong province in Eastern China, one hour flight from Beijing," I replied.

FLYING INTO CHINA – A NEW TERRITORY

I had always been open to go where I was needed and at the time, it was in Qingdao, China. I was excited, yet I had felt some trepidation to go into a new territory. Ben escorted me to Manila. When I lost sight of him in the crowd as I entered the airport terminal, apprehension came over me. "What am I doing? China was not on my list of possible jobs when I decided to help build and develop Shalom Learning School - Going to teach in China? -Well, why not?"

In the waiting section of China Airlines, I struck up a conversation with a Filipino Muslim, who was a customs officer. I learned that he was from Balabagan - a friend of our family and some of his nieces and nephews attend Shalom. Just then my flight was called. He was my last connection to Balabagan before I embarked into an unknown world! The clerk took one look at my travel documents and whisked me through. I found myself seated in the front row of the economy section. Next to me was Steve, a young Swedish engineer who was on his way to North China where his company was building a railroad near the Russian border.

Dinner was served before the airplane landed in Narita Airport in Japan. I had chicken and stir fry vegetables. Steve asked if I needed a fork and spoon. I told him that I had learned to use chopsticks many years ago in Hong Kong. Our conversation turned out to be a good introduction for me about China, its people, its culture, ancient history and cuisine. He advised me that I must take every opportunity to travel and see the vast country.

The next stop from Narita was Shanghai and then the last leg of my travel was to Beijing. Steve spoke fluent Mandarin and promised to help me in Beijing Airport. I told him that I was grateful to have met him on a flight into my unknown.

CHAPTER 15

"You chart the wind ahead of me and tell me where to stop and rest.
You both preceded and follow me and place your hand of blessing on my head.
If I ride the morning winds to the farthest oceans, even there you will guide me.
Your strength will support me." (Psalm 139:2-9 TLB)

QINGDAO INTERNATIONAL SCHOOL

The flight from Manila to Beijing gave me hours to brace myself for challenges and new experiences in a new territory. I went to China to earn funds to develop Shalom Learning School but I was also determined to learn Chinese culture, to meet new people, to break cultural barriers and most of all to be an excellent teacher. Living in China would also give me the opportunity to travel, to come to grips with being a widow and to live again with purpose and joy.

It was dark when the airplane landed in Beijing in the field, and we took the bus to the terminal. It was crowded, just like in Manila. Steve saw a gentleman with the sign, "MUNN" and spoke to him in Mandarin. It was Mr. Liu who was to meet me. I was in good hands Steve assured me and left to catch his connecting flight. Mr. Liu, who spoke good English, said, "Follow me. I have your ticket to Qingdao - one hour flight from here."

We plowed through the crowd. He got my boarding pass, talked on his cell phone, handed it to me and said,

"Here, Mr. Guo wants to talk you." I mumbled, "Who in the world is Mr. Guo?"

It was "Tim" Guo, Executive Director of Qingdao International School (QIS), welcoming me to China and Qingdao.

He said that there would be people to meet me in Qingdao airport. How nice of him to talk to me! It was an impression that led to a close relationship with the Guo family, not only all four years that I was in Qingdao but even today.

At Qingdao airport, Cathy George, the QIS Principal, greeted me with a big smile and a huge flower bouquet! With her were Jessica Liu, the administrative assistant who had been corresponding with me and Jack, the van chauffeur. While Jessica made sure that all my documents were in order, I discovered that Cathy was from Auburn, Washington. Jack drove us to QIS campus, Cathy and Jessica took me to my apartment.

There, for the first time, I was alone. I made coffee and enjoyed it while reflecting on my busy life during the last four months. I felt some trepidation to find myself in a foreign land, but the stillness of the night lulled me to sleepiness. I woke up to a warm August morning in Qingdao, a city of six million people on the shores of the Yellow Sea and across from Korea.

Qingdao International School (QIS) has a landscaped campus overlooking valleys, hills, and the Yellow Sea. Its faculty and staff were from the United States, Canada, Australia, Belgium, Japan and China. It is a private school and Tim Guo's father, George Guo - "Grandpa" was Chairman of the Board.

Classes had already started when I arrived. The English literature teacher in the high school had been substituting for me. She was from Australia. I was pleased to see McGraw-Hill series for reading, math and science. Fifth grade social studies, however, focused on the history of the United States, so I had to organize my own teaching materials for that class.

The fifth grade consisted of five male students – four Koreans and one Chinese. One of them was the son of the Korean Consul in QIngdao. A Korean girl joined the class after a few months into the school year and in the spring, a Japanese girl. I had a full-time assistant, Lisa, a very personable young lady, who spoke good English and was excellent in class. I learned a lot from her, not only about Chinese culture, but about education in Chinese schools. She told me that one way she learned English was singing English songs in school; she said she was in the "John Denver" generation.

Lisa and the children introduced me to an entirely different culture. Lee, the Chinese student, for example, invited his classmates, Lisa, and me to his birthday party in his home. He had warned us that there was going to be a "sha-la-la." I asked, "What is sha-la-la?" "Oh, you know, dancing." He smiled and danced!

Lee's home showed modern day Chinese affluence. During dinner, classical music was played in the background. The food was excellent and Lisa translated all that was going on for me. After dinner, we moved to a spacious living room, decorated with Chinese art and lots of indoor plants. Music started and a handsome gentleman came towards Lisa and me.

She said, "Oh, he will dance with you."

I got on the floor with him and we opened the dance, followed by other couples. He was an excellent dancer and I could have danced all night. That experience in Lee's home was an eye-opening introduction to the side of China which embraced capitalism and enjoyed the freedom of affluence.

TEACHING IS MY PASSION; EDUCATING CHILDREN IS MY CALLING.

I browsed through teaching materials and planned an integrated program of science, math, social studies, reading and elementary English. It opened a whole new world of discovery and invariably improved English proficiency. My students had been fascinated with the solar system, where a city is located using latitude and longitude, why one end of an orange is sweeter than the other end, why plants grow, why egg shells melt in vinegar and so on. We explored such topics and when the science fair was held at the school, they were quite ready.

In my classroom we had a science station - a discovery corner for experiments by individuals and/or teams. They had to read, measure, write observations and give   presentations in class. During winter we dissected fruits, vegetables and fish, and in the spring we planted sunflowers. It became an issue among students why our sunflower plants were tiny, whereas the ones planted by the gardeners were large. Often, we went outdoors for field observation – noticing bees buzzing near flowers, identifying plants, hunting for grasshoppers, rubbing leaves on paper and writing haiku poems to go with them, or singing. Sean Maroney, the computer teacher and I collaborated on research projects and Dan Gosnell, the art teacher, integrated students' haiku poems into their art work.

PANCAKE EGG TRAGEDY

One favorite activity was observing the physical and chemical changes of matter when we made pancakes in the classroom. They observed the physical change of breaking an egg and stirring the baking powder into the batter to prepare for the chemical change that happens during cooking pancakes, and they observed the smell wafting in the room. The batter became pancakes because of physical and chemical changes.

Once, a student accidentally dropped an egg on the tile floor. So, I asked, "How do you pick up a broken egg from the floor?"

Someone came with a broom and a bucket. The incident caused a lot of talking, - yes, in English. However, they were not happy because it was delaying the pancakes.

I said, "Ok, everyone has to watch how I pick up the broken egg because you will have to write a paragraph and read it to class." I took two pieces of bond paper from my desk and scooped it up with those. They were surprised to see that thin paper would hold the mess. I reminded them to write a paragraph. "Oh yes, Mrs. Munn. We will write and share with the class - after we have our pancake."

Later, one girl said, "The title of my story is Tragedy of an Egg."

Everybody looked at her when I said, "Good idea. Why did you think of that?"

"Well, the poor egg is gone forever," she said.

SANTA IS SICK

Qingdao International School reserved the auditorium of the Qingdao Holiday Inn for its annual Christmas program. During my first year I found out that each class had to participate, so I asked my fifth graders what they wanted to do. They decided to present a play, but who would write it? "I will write the play," said Jordan. "The title of the play is 'Santa Is Sick' and everyone will have a role in it."

He came to my desk and told me in a quiet manner what he had in mind. He said,

"Mark cannot sit, so we will make him Santa and he is sick."

Mark was a brilliant student but he was a kinesthetic learner and could not sit down. The other five members of the class tolerated his moving around the room after I explained the difference between kinesthetic and auditory learners. They were auditory learners, whereas Mark was kinesthetic. In Jordan's mind, the only way Mark could be in one place was if he was sick. "Good idea," I told him.

Jordan was a gifted student, but he was more fluent in spoken than written English. He struggled to write the play, and finally, I told him to dictate it to me; I would type it. I was amazed at what he had come up with! Santa is sick and a doctor had to fly to China and take care of sick Santa in Laoshan village the setting of the play. I asked Jordan why a doctor from Minnesota?

He replied, "You know, when we read the story about the Prairie States in the USA, it was so boring, but you told us about the Mayo Clinic in Minnesota and what it does and that was interesting." So the doctor came from Minnesota.

Jordan directed the play and acted as the doctor. The reindeer were Andy and Lee, and Francisco was Elf, Santa's helper. Mark was Santa. Larae made the costumes and the boys designed and painted the scenery.

Although Julie, the only girl in class, did not want to be on stage, she finally agreed to participate as Narrator, but only if she were hidden behind the podium and plants. Of course, she did very well and so did everyone else. Their parents were very proud!

The success of the play set a tone for succeeding fifth grade classes, so that each Christmas thereafter, the fifth grade class always presented a play, written by them, and parents expected their children to perform on stage when they reached the fifth grade.

THE MAGIC OF MUSIC

I found music is also an effective tool to learn English. During my second year at QIS, I started teaching my students American folk songs and some songs from the "Sound of Music." Also, I used singing to quiet them down. I would just stand in front of class, and the students knew it was a signal for singing. We would start with "Clementine," sing other songs and always end with "Shenandoah." When mothers came for parties, they were always thrilled to hear the students sing, and during Christmas, this class led in the singing of carols in the QIS foyer.

There were seventeen children in my class during my last year at QIS. The "Fifth Grade Singers," was invited to teach English songs to children in a nearby Chinese school. Every Friday afternoon a school bus would take us. The QIS students were proud and happy to reach out and to teach English songs there.

HAIKU POETRY

Searching for more ideas to enrich students' learning of the English language, I had found that writing Haiku was a simple, quick and a creative activity. We started with simple, descriptive thoughts, but gradually I taught them haiku with deeper meaning. I encouraged them to write about their trips using haiku poems.

After they had written several haiku poems, I would take the class outdoors to rub leaves on paper and then write their poems on their paper with leaf designs. They wrote words over the rubbed design and made into their own book. With a simplified lesson on "publishing" students learned to write and publish.

Many mornings I would write a first line. Throughout the day students would figure out the other two lines and share at the end of day. Then as a class, they would write the day's class poem, which we copied for each student. These were compiled into a haiku poetry book, written by them and dedicated to their parents. Individual and class haiku poetry books were displayed during "QIS Festival of Writing."

I myself became intrigued with expressing my thoughts about China and my travels through haiku. I published Moon River on Qingdao Bay - my own haiku book. Jessica Liu, who was also a Chinese language teacher, translated the poems into Chinese, Dan Gosnell, the art teacher, formatted the book and a local publishing.

THE SOLAR SYSTEM

I told the class that we would make a planetarium. The solar system gave everyone a good research topic, and each student did research during their class in the computer room. The computer skills teacher, Sean Maroney, was passionate about the subject, so he and I collaborated on the project.

Students were grouped and assigned to make a planet by blowing up balloons, covering them with paper mache and painting them according to planet colors as shown in the encyclopedia or on the internet. Then the class laid out huge piece of paper on the floor and painted the planets' orbits in oval fashion. Each planet was pinned where it is located in relation to other planets.

I told the children that we would hang this up on the ceiling and asked them to figure out how to do it. John said, "It will rip in no time." I told him he was right, and others made comments, but finally, John said,

"Oh Mrs. Munn, there is no way we can hang it up."

However, Leo, my assistant and I had already figured out what to do. He took out a white bed sheet and ropes. I had Leo explain to the class what we would do.

"Roll this paper from the floor to the wall. We will spread out the bed sheet on the floor and unroll the paper back over it. Ok, everybody pin this paper on the bed sheet." That process took a long time, but it provided the class an opportunity to converse only in English. When they were done, Leo tied a rope on each corner of the bed sheet and then two men came to hang the "Fifth Grade Planetarium" from the ceiling. The colorful balloons hung above the classroom. The children were proud to tell friends from other classes to come and see the "planetarium" which remained up on the ceiling the rest of the semester.

In addition to teaching fifth grade, I also taught Spanish after school for two years and Indian bead work for two years. The children were fascinated and especially interested in making necklaces and earrings and even sold them during the QIS bazaar.

Also, Qingdao International School had an "English Corner," a school outreach to the community. It was held in a MacDonald's restaurant in JUSCO, one of the supermarkets, owned by Japanese. Four teachers went at a time; each took a table, and people of all ages came around for English conversation. I usually spread a map of the United States for everyone to see. Visitors' questions elicited lots of discussion and more questions.

Two popular questions were, "Where is Harvard University? Where is Stanford University?" Many asked questions about how to get admission in colleges and universities, but also how I went to America from the Philippines. And they liked to ask, "What do you like in America?"

I looked forward to these sessions because I was learning a lot about Chinese culture and attitudes. We talked about life in the village, in the city, people, customs, traditions and food. They asked if I liked Chinese food and this discussion led me to visit a noodle factory. I had observed, I commented to them that Chinese had come to like hamburgers: there was always a crowd in MacDonalds. One man said, "We also like Kentucky fried chicken." (There was a Kentucky Fried Chicken restaurant in CARRE FOUR, a French supermarket in Qingdao.)

At the end of each morning session, each of us was compensated with MacDonald's hamburger, fries, an "apple pie," and coffee. What a treat to have a hamburger!

WORK VACATIONS IN SHALOM LEARNING SCHOOL

All the planning and activities kept me active and focused on the present and near future. Yet, China's proximity to the Philippines made it possible for me to go home to Balabagan during QIS school vacations. Each time I was home, it was always a work vacation. I continued to observe classrooms, to help teachers by offering workshops in curriculum and classroom management, to hold teacher conferences, and to assess building projects for SLS. It was the reason why I was in China – to earn funds to develop the school.

Teaching in China was also giving me the challenges and rewards so that my life was moving on, and it renewed my self confidence and zest for living. The opportunity had come suddenly, and I was determined to seize whatever it was I could learn about the people and the country. I thought that I must travel as much as I could. As Mert used to say, "Travel when you can to enrich your life"

CHAPTER 16

"You are my hiding place from every storm of my life;
You even keep me from getting into trouble!
You surround me with songs of victory."
(Psalm 32:7 TLB)

WHISPERING BAMBOO GROVES

I embarked on my sojourn in China determined to learn all that I could about the people and the country – the places where I worked, the immediate environs and famous Chinese places near and far. I also found a vibrant international community in Qingdao and that added to opportunities to mix cultures. I began my transition from a bereaved widow to a woman with expectations for a future: one can live with memories, yet go forward with life.

The "Autumn Festival" begins on the 15th day of the 8th month, usually in September, and marks the end of the harvest in China. It is celebrated with the "Chinese National Holiday" and schools are on vacation. It is also known as "Moon Festival" because the moon is at its roundest, as my Chinese friends say. Families gather to appreciate the bright full moon, to eat moon cakes (sweet round pastries) and think of loved ones who are far away. Lovers who are separated by distance look at the full moon and visit with each other in silence.

A day during that vacation, Jessica and I decided to climb Lao Shan, a thousand foot ascent in a village near Qingdao. We took a taxi, but before we reached the entrance to the park, the driver stopped on the roadside and hailed a man in a motorcycle. Jessica stepped out in a flash and got on that motorcycle! I was stunned, alone in this taxi in the middle of nowhere, and I did not know what was going on. The driver got back on the road and off we went. There, on the other side of the Park Entrance, Jessica was all smiles, waiting for me. What she did helped the taxi driver so he wouldn't pay more at the Park Entrance because I was a foreigner. I did not understand it all but I was "in for the ride" and to enjoy whatever the day would bring.

Near the Information Center are gigantic ancient gingko trees. Then, I called Jessica's attention to a sign at the door which said, "50% for Seniors."

Stunned, she asked, "Why, how old are you?"

Grinning, I replied, "I am 63 years old."

"Oh my! Are you still going to climb the mountain?" she countered.

"Yes, of course! I am fine. I can do it." I assured her.

I had not climbed mountains since I was a child during World War II but I did not tell her this. The steps on Lao Shan ("shan" means mountain) were narrow but short and easy to navigate with my short legs. That is, the first three hundred feet were easy, but I wasn't used to climbing a lot and it became harder and harder. When I was feeling tired along the way, I could not tell Jessica, but I'd say, "Let us stop and listen to the silent whispers of bamboo groves."

"I am listening but it is so quiet. I don't hear anything," she said.

"Oh, but you can hear the whispers. Soft, gentle breeze you can feel, and see the slight movement of bamboo dancing in the sunlight." I said.

The brief rest in the bamboo groves buoyed up my spirit and soon I was ready to climb again. One time, two men came by with a chair strung on bamboo poles carried on their shoulders. Jessica explained that for a fee, one can ride in it up or down the mountain. It was also used in case of emergency. She assured me that it was very safe and that there was never an accident of falling off the mountain. With the narrow path, I wondered, I braced myself and was determined not to faint as I climbed. The last 100 feet were most difficult: I had to consciously tell one foot to get in front of the other.

We finally made it to the top and it was worth the climb! It is a lifetime experience to see the panoramic view surrounding Lao Shan and the distant Yellow Sea that separates Qingdao from Korea. Up there we explored a rock cave, the darkness illumined only by sunlight through a crack in the rock. By the time we were out of the cave, I was very tired and hungry. It was a relief to see food vendors. We had noodles and fruit.

Descending from Lao Shan would take hours and I really did not know if my legs could carry me down. Neither would I dare ride the bamboo chair carried by two men. It was mid-afternoon and Jessica said, "There is a cable car to ride down but it is expensive, $3.00 each."

"Let's take it." I said. A sudden burst of energy lifted me up from where I was sitting on a rock; I almost sprinted to the cable car. Then, we took a taxi back to Qingdao in time for dinner at the cafeteria.

The following day in class I told my students about the wonderful experience I had had. And I learned that another famous mountain that our teachers, staff, and students like to climb is Tai Shan. Traveling there requires an overnight stay in that area and I told them that I would like to do it someday.

Jordan said, "Oh no, Mrs. Munn, you will never make it."

A DAY IN A VILLAGE PARK

I didn't ever go to Tai Shan but with Tim, Wendy, his wife and QIS teachers. I went to a village - more like a park --- with trees, stream and white boulders. I followed Wendy, who was pregnant; she crossed the stream on a rock path very carefully. We enjoyed the sights on the other side of the stream but instead of retracing the path with Wendy, I followed a bunch of young people climbing huge boulders. I quickly realized that I did not have their long legs or their physical stamina to go over enormous and tall boulders. But they helped me up. Peter, up on the rock, pulled me up while Tamara and Stephanie pushed me up. This maneuver took quite a while which was quite a scene for the rest of our group watching on the other side. Wendy and Tim and the rest of them were just all smiles and when I joined them Tim handed me a bamboo cane. He had bought a bunch of them and distributed to all the women. The canes - a kind thought on Tim's part - did not single me out as the only one who needed one. It was such a pleasant day, but I had to remember that my legs were short and that my age had started to show.

Tim took us all out to lunch in a village restaurant. The food was wonderful but we had to taste some delicacies, like fried insects. Hunger can give you the courage to eat just about anything.

At the beginning of the 2003-2004 school year, I was perplexed all week. The second installment on the classroom construction at Shalom Learning School was due that week and payday was not till the end of the month. I needed $2,400 to send to the Philippines. One day, Tim asked if Fei Fei, a girl from Shanghai, could live with me so I could tutor her in English. She would come as an eighth grader. Readily, I said, "Yes, I would love to have her. When is she coming?"

"Next week, and oh, the parents will pay you for tutoring her," he replied.

"Oh no, they need not pay me. You are already giving me free board and an apartment." I said. He left, but the following day, he came back and handed me a thick white envelope and said,

"Fei Fei's parents insist that they pay you $600 a month. Here's $2,400 for the first four months." He left and I counted 24 crisp $100 bills! Yes! My prayers were answered! I was so thankful, and even more so because I had almost interfered with receiving it.

Tall and beautiful, Fei Fei was a fast learner. Within a few months with me, her English proficiency accelerated to a much higher level. I told Tim that she would no longer need my tutoring the following year but I would be available to help with school work. (Fei Fei graduated from the University of California-Irvine in 2011.) Kevin, Fei Fei's friend also from Shanghai, would sometimes join us. He lived with a Canadian couple upstairs. (Kevin graduated from the University of Toronto in 2013.)

Climbing mountains, huge boulders and the Great Wall taught me limits to what my physical body could do but the experience also taught me that It was always worth taking the challenge. I had, however, realized that I could still enjoy those episodes by helping young people see the beauty of it all, as I did with Fei Fei and Kevin in the spring after SARS was controlled.

SARS (Severe Acute Respiratory Syndrome) hammered China during most of Year 2003. The spread of this deadly epidemic curtailed travel but in the spring of 2004 it was considered safe to go places. Qingdao International School's vacation was in the first week of April and I planned to visit my friend, Jessica in Beijing.

On a clear Saturday, Fei Fei and I would usually spend the day at the beach, but this day, it was raining so we stayed home to watch "The Princess Diary." We were also eating pomelo – a huge grapefruit with green skin and the size of a soccer ball, when Fei Fei said,

"Mrs. Munn, where are you going for spring vacation?"

"I am going to Beijing. Why?" I replied.

"Oh, can I go with you? I have not been to Beijing!" she exclaimed. She bounced up from the couch with excitement.

I said, "Oh, I don't know, SARS is still going on. You will have to ask permission from your parents."

"Oh, they will let me go, I am sure. Can Kevin go too?"

That would mean not only one, but two. However, they were very nice kids and I decided that I did not mind taking them to Beijing.

"You have to talk to Mr. Tim Guo about this. You and Kevin go to him." I told her.

Well, I did not know what they told Tim, but two days later, he came and said, "Yes, Fei Fei and Kevin can go with you to Beijing. I just talked to their parents in Shanghai."

Kevin was overjoyed! He had never been to Beijing either. I told them that Jessica would stay with us in the hotel and would be our guide. They already knew her from QIS.

"Oh, I want to stay in a 5-Star hotel," Kevin said.

I looked at him and said, "Oh no, Kevin, I don't stay in 5-Star hotels, but where we will stay, you will be there, too."

He said "Okay" with pouting lips but I knew that deep inside he was happy. He was a nice and respectful 14-year old.

As it turned out it was good that these two young people went with me to Beijing because Jessica wanted them to listen to my haiku, which she had translated into Chinese. So, Jessica joined us in the hotel and in the evenings she read the poems and had them critique her translation.

It was springtime and daylight started very early. When light came through cracks of drapes, I knew it was going to be a beautiful day. Suddenly, Kevin bounced out of bed and said,

"Wake up, wake up, it is time to get going. Let's have breakfast."

I told them to have a good breakfast because it was going to be a long day. Jessica would take us on a tour to the Great Wall, the Summer Palace, the Ming Tombs and end in the

Forbidden City. I had been on these tours previously, but I had enjoyed them and would take this opportunity to go again.

"Where are we going to have lunch?" they asked.

I said, "It all depends on where we will be by noon."

Off we went to the bus stop, destination the Great Wall. The bus door opened, Kevin, Fei Fei and I rushed in. The bus departed and I turned, but Jessica was not with us!

"Oh, my, I thought," and she was our tour guide. At the destination, we waited for the next bus and when it stopped, there was Jessica! She had wanted to tell us to take the next bus because it was cheaper but we got in too quickly and the door had closed by the time she got there.

We bought our tickets at the entrance and walked to the Great Wall. Kevin yelled "Come on, Mrs. Munn, let's go" and he took the steps as light as a feather!

Kevin was so excited! Fei Fei with her long legs was right with him. Right then and there, I realized that I could never go at their pace. I told them to climb as far as they wanted, but I would go at my own pace and I would wait for them. Jessica also went farther up.

One thing with climbing is that one has to eventually come down. For short legged-people like me, that is not easy. There were times on the steps of Great Wall when I would be tempted to negotiate going down "toddler style" - sitting down on the step, lowering my bottom to the next and so on. However, I did not dare!

When I could no longer see Fei Fei and Kevin through a long snake of people climbing and walking the Great Wall, I knew that they had gone beyond the Second Tower. I decided to start my return. I had picked up one foot at a time and lowered the other in a civilized fashion. I got to the bottom and waited.

Soon, Jessica also descended. I told her how magnificent the Great Wall was!

"Yes," she said, "made by millions of men many, many years ago." I just sat there looking at the city of Beijing spread far beyond and listened to her stories. I had to pinch myself for this chance to be viewing an ancient seat of civilization. I was rested and about noon, Fei Fei and Kevin arrived.

"How was it?" I said.

"Wonderful!" Fei Fei said.

"It was great, Mrs. Munn, but I am hungry." Kevin said. We took the bus to the Summer Palace and had lunch there.

The Palace is along a lake in a huge park of temples, gardens, pavilions and a 700 meter "Long Corridor" decorated with paintings of mythical scenes. A marble boat sits immobile on the edge of the lake. We climbed a few hundred steps to the "Benevolence Longevity Hall" but it was worth the climb to see the view. The Summer Palace was my favorite respite whenever I was on a Beijing tour.

We skipped the Ming Tombs and went directly to Wangfujing, the shopping district. The next day we toured the Forbidden City, the largest and best-preserved cluster of ancient Chinese buildings. I had fun telling Fei Fei and Kevin about it.

Kevin said, "Where did you learn about this?"

"I read a lot, and I love history," I told him. I had read and heard about the ancient sites of Chinese history and visiting them always made me pinch myself to be sure that I knew that I was not stepping on those "hallowed" grounds.

We flew back to Qingdao the following morning, and when I returned from Beijing, I promised myself to see more of China.

CHAPTER 17

"Fix your thoughts on what is true and good and right.
Think about things that are pure and lovely, and
dwell on fine, good things in others." (Philippians 4:8 TLB)

MOON RIVER ON QINGDAO BAY

Sightseeing in China was more enjoyable because I toured with people I knew. I had explored Qingdao itself with my young friends at QIS. The city takes pride in its Bavarian appearance and Tsingtao Beer - living legacy of the German occupation in the early 1900's. Along the bay is a long board walk, a romantic promenade. Once, in late spring, I sat on a bench on the board walk and witnessed the red fireball sunset finally disappearing on the horizons. The rising moon started to shimmer on the ocean, inspiring my book of haikus, Moon River on Qingdao Bay.

QUFU: CONFUCIUS SHRINE

I visited Confucius Shrine with a friend from the United States. The Shrine, Confucius birthplace, is in Qufu, eighty-one kilometers from Jinan, the capital of Shandong province. It is a daytime or an overnight trip from Qingdao.

My friend and I took the overnight train. We occupied a "Soft Sleeper"- berth on the train with double bunk beds. Sharing the berth with us were a mother and her daughter on their way to Beijing. The leg room between two double bunk beds was tight, and on one end was a pot of hot water, typical on train berths for passengers to use for coffee or tea. A friend in QIS told me about it so I came prepared with mugs, coffee, and tea. She was right! My friend and I had our coffee and chatted in low voices as our roommates were getting ready to sleep. Then we went to bed. In the night I could hear the train chugging along and the lady across from us snorIng all night.

I was awakened by a tap on my shoulder and a gentle voice said, "I will see you in the dining car." It was early morning.

It was a sunny autumn day. In Yanzhou train station we took a van to the Shrine. There was a hotel in the midst of many buildings and it had a restaurant. My friend said, "Let's have breakfast before the tour guide comes."

"We already had breakfast on the train," I replied.

"It will be a long day of hiking – lots of things to see, but no food," my friend said.

So, we had our second breakfast.

The guide announced that there were nine gates to go through and the tour would require a lot of walking. I did not mind walking because along the way there were lots of colorful pavilions, marble columns, ancient courtyards and tall evergreen trees. (They reminded me of home in Washington State.) I was so impressed with the row of stone tablets (stele) on which were etched pictures and the written story of Confucius life. Imprints of these tablets are made on special Chinese paper. Women buff each tablet before rubbing on it and then they pass the paper to a person who, with a magnifying glass, makes the lines more visible. I enjoyed watching the reproduction process and I wanted to buy, but imprints were not sold on the site.

The pavilions dating back to the Ming Dynasty are made of wood. I said to my friend, "These pavilions are so old and well preserved. No termites?"

"It is too cold in this country for termites," my friend replied.

The guide took us to the Confucian Forest – over 100,000 pine and cypress trees in an area of 200 hectares (about 500 acres). We had to ride a vehicle powered by electricity to cover the four kilometer (2.5 mile) perimeter of the tombs – earth mounds, like hills – a cemetery for Confucius and all his descendants.

In the evening, my friend and I watched performers dance in colorful costumes. Then we walked to lighted tents down the road. Those turned out to be roadside eating tents with tables of ingredients on display to be cooked right in front of guests. The man did the cooking in just one wok, rinsing it after each dish was done. His wife washed dishes in basins filled from buckets of water. There were two small tables inside. We were the only guests within the two hours that we were there. The food was delicious, but I wondered how they could earn enough.

We took the train back to Qingdao during the day on a "Soft Seater," – having cushioned chairs with comfortable backs. The train chugged through countryside scattered with farms and plant nurseries. What a wonderful and relaxing trip! I was forever grateful to my friend for this enjoyable and perfect three-day historical tour.

A TOUR IN THE WINTER

I travelled to Beijing, Chongqing, Shanghai, and Xian with my niece, Bing Rivera from Perth, Western Australia. A graduate of Silliman University, Bing earned her Master's Degree in Oregon State University and immigrated to Australia. I had just won a prize at the Qingdao Winter Ball; the prize was "2 Nights for 2 at the Traders Hotel" in Beijing. Our third night, at Bing's request, we stayed in a hutong hotel – a single level building in a hutong (narrow alleyway) settlement whIch preserves a sense of togetherness – neighbors knowing and helping each other.

In addition to historical places, Bing and I also enjoyed visiting jade and pearl factories, and the Chinese medicine shops. At these, tourists were invited to rooms where doctors examined us and wrote prescriptions that were filled in the pharmacy. There, in large glass-covered shelves, were displays of sources of medicine – herbs, tree roots, bark, skins, hair, oil, and so on.

For lunch, we saw dozens of tour buses with hundreds of people stopped in front of an enormous building. Inside were large round tables set for lunch. Bing and I were cautious what food to put on our plates. There was one that we did not touch – a perfectly scallop-shaped meat. After lunch during another tour we saw live chickens in cages, and we realized that those perfect scallop-shapes were chicken coxcombs, all cleaned and sautéed. I was sure they tasted good, just like the chicken feet that we enjoyed.

One highlight of our Beijing tour was attending the Chinese opera, "Stealing the Emperor's Horse."

"Down the hill to the valley in the moonlight,
Look out carefully and get the horse; I will ride on it."

The lead was performed by a man in a "jing actor role" – in painted face, representing warrior, hero and an adventurer. The archaic Chinese was dubbed from a screen above the proscenium. Screeching music was hard on the ears, the swift battle sequences with acrobats twirling, twisting and somersaulting were challenging to the eyes and ears. The costumes were vibrant. It was a breath-taking experience.

Bing had experienced winter in the USA and she was thrilled to walk in Tiananmen Square under falling snow. At the Ming Tombs, a lady was sweeping snow with a broom. At the Summer Palace, the willow trees were all white! Beijing was blanketed in snow when our plane took off for Chongqing.

We flew to Chongqing in southwestern China to a completely different weather; it was warm and sunny. The Yangtze River cruises started from there. The building of the Three Gorges Dam was in progress, but already, thousands of people had been relocated to the city from villages along the Yangtze River. Displaced people crowded Chongqing, a city built on steep hills; the population surged to more than 30 million. A business boom was evident and foreigners were relocating there as well. Why did we go Chongqing? A Chinese friend suggested that I should open an international school there. The idea was good and it would have been a challenge, but it required $150,000 initial investment.

We toured historical sites in Chongqing, especially those prominently used by the government during World War II. The public square with a gigantic artificial snowman was crowded with people. At the dockside, we had lunch in a restaurant and watched boats start downriver. These cruises were drastically changed later when Three Gorges Dam opened.

Bing wanted to see pandas but winter is not a good time to go to Chengdu Panda Reserve in Sichuan Province, so we went to the zoo in Shanghai to see them. Also in Shanghai, we enjoyed shopping and milling with people on Nanjing Road, and resting in a Starbucks Coffee Shop.

In our hotel room, overlooking the dazzling lights of Shanghai, we discussed at length my reason for working in China and the future of Shalom Learning School. As a board member, Bing initiated and had helped develop the school's strategic plan and my role was making the plan happen. She and I had read "The Magic of Thinking Big," and yes, we had big dreams for Shalom.

I had heard and read about the famous Terra Cotta Warriors. Bing had planned also to see for herself what her co-worker in Perth had described. We flew to Xian the following day.

TERRA COTTA WARRIORS IN BATTLE FORMATION

Xian is the capital of Shaanxi province and home to the "Terra Cotta Warriors Museum." A nephew of Bing's co-worker in Perth met us at the airport and escorted us on our tour. Bing and I met the farmer on whose property the vaults of statues were discovered; he was in the Museum, signing books. It took us many hours to look and move around the perimeter to view this display of 7,000 life-size warriors, who were guardsmen of the ancient emperor's tomb.

Emperor Qin Shi Huang, the first Qin Dynasty emperor of China, was only thirteen years old when he ascended the throne. He started building his tomb at a very young age, and inside the tomb were palaces of precious stones. He defeated his enemies, united the country and ruled for 36 years. His rule ended at his death at 49 years old; his successor son held on for four years, but then the Qin Dynasty fell to the Han Dynasty.

Two years after Bing visited, my friends Mary June Hertel and Phil and Carol Thayer from Spokane were in Beijing. We arranged to meet in Xian for their tour of the Terra Cotta Warriors Museum. It was my second visit, but I never ceased to wonder at the immense creation of hundreds of life-size warrior statues! What was on the mind of Emperor Qin? In ancient times, Xian was the gateway of the Silk Road - the commerce and trade route with India and countries further west, leaving in its wake some Muslim influence in the area. Mary June and I went shopping in the Muslim market. I was struck by similarities of brass wares that are found in Lanao del Sur, my home province in the Philippines.

PLACES HITHER AND YON

When Judy Zappone, my neighbor in Medical Lake came to visit, Lisa and I took Judy to Zhongdian (Shangri-la), the last city in China near the Tibet- China border in Yunnan province. We had to fly to Liqiang and take the bus from there. A great part of the city was rebuilt after an earthquake but the old town is still a maze of shops. It had cobbled streets with gushing canals of clear water alongside and many restaurants. I saw a sign in Korean on a restaurant door and we decided to have dinner there. The food was great but the greatest surprise was strawberry-rhubarb pie on the menu! We ordered pie a la mode (with ice cream). This was all new to Lisa but she liked this American dessert. The Korean lady met her Chinese husband while they were students in New York City.

The following day we took the bus to Zhongdian, home to ethnic Naxi – descendants of the Tibetan Qiang tribe. Along the way, I was so thrilled to see the first bend of the Yangtze River in Sheigu and the Tiger Leaping Gorge, one of the deepest gorges in the world. I sat on a marble seat under a granite overhang along

151

the gorge and just listened to the sound of water, "leaping" toward its destination!

The bus rumbled along for a long time but then had to stop behind lines of buses. A huge boulder that had fallen on the road was being cleared. So we waited. Spring rains had turned the hillside into all shades of green. Then, rows of colorful umbrellas on the hillside caught my attention, I said, "Lisa, look at those umbrellas up there."

She smiled, and said, "If you want to go 'bathroom,' here's an umbrella." I could only smile. Soon afterwards, the traffic began to move.

In Zhongdian, we were ushered into an entertainment building. At the entrance, a greeter placed a white silk scarf around my neck, a gesture of welcome. Inside was a huge rectangular hall with seats along the sides and an open space in the center. In front of our seats were long tables with food and drink. I said to Judy, "Be careful what you eat and drink. It is kind of dark here."

I picked up the smallest cup and took a sip. It was Tibetan whiskey! It burned my throat."

"What did you drink, Mrs. Munn?" Lisa inquired.

Judy turned to her and said, "She had whiskey," and laughed.

The waiters were all dressed in colorful native costumes. Music started, and Lisa said, "Come on, Mrs. Munn! Let us join in their Tibetan line dancing."

I got right in the swing of it and had a marvelous time! Was it the whiskey in me? Judy just sat there quietly taking it all in – the crowd, the noise and the music. Each tour bus had to have a "singer" sing to the crowd. There were people from Malaysia, Indonesia, and Singapore. All sang songs in Chinese! Lisa had told the tour guide that I was a Filipino from America. She bounced right back to our seats and said, "Mrs. Munn, they want you to sing a song in English."

I said, "Sure, I will." I went down to the center and sang, "The Way We Were." The hall filled with tourists was quiet. Suddenly, I could not remember lyrics to the last part of the song. I just repeated what I remembered more than once, and said, "Xi Xi" (Thank you)

Soon, my neck was lost in layers and layers of white silk scarves, which many gave in appreciation.

En route to the hotel that night, I led in the singing, including "Wo Ai Ni" a Chinese love song. Some people knew American folk songs. Their favorite was "You Are my Sunshine."

Someone asked, "Are you American?"

"Yes, I am," I replied.

"But you are Filipino?"

"Yes, I am Filipino-American." I had to do some explaining.

We flew back to Qingdao. On the plane, I said to Lisa, "I read about a cave - a very large cave - that was used during World War II as shelter from Japanese air raids."

"Oh, do you want to go? It is in Guilin. I'll take you there next year."

I took Judy to Beijing for a few days. Jessica joined us on the tour. On our last day there, Judy and I went shopping in Wangfujing. It was hot, so we decided to return to our hotel but while waiting for a taxi, many motorized cabs surrounded us. The drivers kept offering a ride to Judy – they did not bother me, I looked like a native. Blond and tall, she stood out in the crowd. One driver kept following her and asking where she was going.

She said, "To the Airport!" I just about keeled over laughing!

We flew back to Qingdao. School year had ended and I took Judy to the Philippines before returning to the United States. We spent a week in Dumaguete. In Malatapay I showed her some fishermen brought in their net of small anchovies and told her that I would buy some for dinner. Her eyes went big! "How do you eat that?" She asked.

My brother, Ben and I gave her a tour of Silliman University and sights along the coast. We had her taste the water from fresh, young coconut and had her eat the tender meat. A week later, she and I flew to San Francisco to visit my niece. We rented a car for the drive to Corvallis, Oregon to pick up my van, which I always left with Gideon and Rachel.

MEDICAL LAKE HOME FOR THE SUMMER

All the travels and intermittent work vacations in Balabagan, in addition to my teaching, in Qingdao, kept me hopping all over throughout the year.

So, it was nice to come home to Medical Lake and to rest. Still, it took me quite awhile to adjust. According to tax rules, I could stay in the USA not more than 35 days of the year. So for tax purposes, my home was in Qingdao and I was just on a brief vacation in Medical Lake. Yet, it was truly my home, my place to rest.

This time, it also struck me that I still missed Mert, even nine years after he died. With that in mind, I was even more determined to make use of my time productively. I planned to teach one more year in China and enjoy last fling of travel in that vast country and to visit my sister, Fely in Queensland, Australia before leaving Qingdao.

CHAPTER 18

"He waters the furrows with abundant rain.....causing seeds to sprout
across the land.
He crowns it all with green, lush pastures in the wilderness.
Hillsides blossom with joy.....valleys are carpeted with green."
(Psalm 65:10-11 TLB)

THE HEALING EFFECT OF TRAVEL AND CULTURAL IMMERSION

I was back in Qingdao in mid-August 2004 just a few days before school started. There were seventeen students in my class, many of them Koreans but others were from Israel, Scandinavia, Canada, Japan, Australia and China. It was going to be a great year, I thought, as I enjoyed a cup of coffee sitting on my favorite rock in the QIS garden. I was really at home and content.

Parents of my students were in Qingdao on business or on government assignment from their country. They were supportive and quite often would come to our classroom to celebrate birthdays, including my 67th. birthday. Our Asian cultures give very high respect for old age, and in Qingdao, I enjoyed that appreciation.

One day, I told my assistant Leo, that I had taken the bus from downtown. He asked, "Well, did somebody give you a seat?"

"No, I had to hang on to a post. The bus was crowded." I said.

Leo said, "You know why nobody offered you a seat? You look young, that's why," I smiled.

That "Autumn Festival" vacation, I had decided to stay home to write my book. The campus was deserted. Except for security guards and a few kitchen staff, everybody had gone home to celebrate with families or travel. I was in misery all week from a chronically swollen foot. A doctor friend told me to elevate my foot, take Naproxen, and take coffee or tea (diuretics) and lots of water to reduce swelling. So, I grabbed my bamboo cane and hobbled to the kitchen to make coffee. Just then Nancy, the cleaning lady saw me. She was horrified! Everyone had assumed that I was traveling.

Nancy learned that all weekend I had had only peanut butter, crackers and nuts, so she reported my condition to the office. Soon kitchen staff started delivering three meals a day to my apartment. The nurse checked on me and a massage lady came daily. A huge floral arrangement from the Guo family was delivered. Tim's mother, "Grandma" visited almost daily and his father, "Grandpa" came a few times. Wow! Such kindness and I truly felt that I was among friends and family.

CULTURAL IMMERSION

Although teaching and living in Qingdao had given me opportunities to travel and be totally immersed in Chinese culture, the language was very difficult to learn. I had had four teachers during the years. Still, I could say only a few words and phrases well.

Yet, I never missed an opportunity to be with people and to participate in events and functions, which gave me a chance to learn more about their culture. Our music teacher invited me to sing with the Qingdao University Chorale. There is no Symphony in Qingdao, so sometimes I spent a weekend in Beijing to attend the China National Symphony. All ages – children, youth, adults and old people were attending and admiring classical music. Once, I invited Jessica to a concert of the symphony. (Jessica had moved to Beijing from Qingdao where she had lived with her parents and worked at QIS.) It was her first concert.

Some weeks later, in one of her phone calls, she said, "I am inviting you and Patti to my parents' home for lunch."

"That will be nice! When will you be arriving?" I replied.

"Oh, I will not be there but my family wants to have you and Patti." She said. I was surprised, but this was a Chinese way.

Patti was a lovely blond lady from Michigan, who taught English as a Second Language, and she was fluent in Chinese. Jessica's family prepared a very delicious lunch. After we ate, Patti said to me, "They want to know if you are a Christian,"

"Oh yes, I am! Why?" I replied.

"They asked if you would please sing a Christian hymn for them," she said.

"Oh, I would be happy to." I replied. "I will sing 'What a Friend We Have in Jesus,' an old hymn." So I did! They asked me to sing it again. After the second time, I told Patti, "Ask them to sing it with me in Chinese." The sound was incredible! We sang it a few more times. What a touching experience!

My favorite shopping place in Qingdao was the public market to wheel and deal over jade and pearls. Cora, my first Chinese teacher, took me there a few times, but she'd always say, "Just look, listen, and do not talk, or they will raise the price." When Cora completed her Master's degree in Business

Administration (MBA) "online" from Columbia Southern University in Alabama, the University hired her to write online programs and she could live in China. She moved to Sanya, Hainan Province, where the climate was warmer. On a cold October morning, Cora called, "Miss Eufemia, you must come to Sanya and spend Thanksgiving with me." Who could resist an invitation to a warmer place during the cold winter in Qingdao?

It was a long flight to Hainan Dao, China's paradise island. Entrance to the city was an avenue of palms and purple bougainvilleas blooming profusely. Cora and I walked on the soft, white sand under blue skies in the shores of an emerald sea. We took naps in a hammock tied to coconut trees at the beach. She took me to Yalong Bay where I bought pearls but what made that trip special was interacting with people in the ethnic village. Sanya had many restaurants where we often ate, but our day always ended at the Sheraton Hotel. There we had dessert and coffee while listening to a Filipino band. It was a wonderful break! I will always cherish Cora's wonderful hospitality.

I always traveled with Chinese companions and this gave me an opportunity to learn more about their lives, their hopes, their thinking, and who they were. I wanted to see more of China and I told Lisa of my wish to visit a cave which was a famous air raid shelter from Japanese war planes during World War II.

Lisa arranged the trip. Lisa, her mom, Gloria and I went on the Li Jiang Cruise to Guilin in Guangxi province. I was thrilled to discover that we were with a small group of women who were on a "mother-daughter" tour.

In Guilin, we started by going to the Reed Flute Cave. Its name comes from reeds growing at the entrance and around this humongous cave. Reed flute music and multicolored stalagmites, stalactites and rocks welcomed us into this ancient cave of natural limestone.   Artificial lights brought out interesting rock formations.   One of them is the "Crystal Palace of the Dragon King," an area that alone can comfortably hold one thousand people. Actually, the cave is under several hectares of land with a very high ceiling. The cave is so big that it served as an air raid shelter from Japanese war planes and as the headquarters of the "Flying Tigers" during World War II.

Lisa said, "We will take a boat trip to Yangshou."   We rejoined our group of women on the Cruise. The boat trip from Guilin to Yangshou took three hours, passing through karst (limestone) peaks, bamboo groves, and countryside landscapes. Some of the women sat with us at the table. They soon found out that, although I looked Chinese, I was a foreigner. They watched me closely. At our lunch of tea eggs, steamed buns, tea and fruit, they were commenting approvingly on how I peeled the tea egg and how I split the steamed bun. They nodded and smiled at me.

In Yangshou, we took a bamboo raft upstream into the Zhangsha tribal region. Ahead of us, a girl rowed a boat and sang a folk song, welcoming us into a forest canyon and to an exquisite waterfall.   Then, back for dinner in a restaurant in the city, we walked by a display of huge jars and inside one, there was a perfectly coiled preserved snake.   This restaurant served snake dishes. One of the ladies said, "Snake is very delicious." It may be, I thought, but I just couldn't eat it! Instead I chose a dish of fried chicken drumsticks.

What made this tour most interesting and meaningful to me was observing the culture and interacting with the people on the tour.

TRADITIONS AND CUSTOMS

I found that in China, there are two major traditions and customs --- the "Mid-Autumn Festival" and the "Chinese New Year." It was quite a celebration with family and friends. I had been invited by the Guo family to a Chinese New Year dinner. Jack, their chauffeur, had picked me up from the apartment and en route, picked up a gentleman I had not seen before. He sat in the front. He did not introduce himself but spoke to me in perfect English. I said,

"You sound like someone who has lived overseas."

"What is 'overseas'?" he replied.

"Abroad," I said. Silence fell and I let it go at that.

Jack drove us to an elegant restaurant. This gentleman and I were ushered into a special room, and there was the Guo family – "Grandpa," "Grandma," Tim, his wife Wendy, their son Little George and Wendy's son John who was in my fifth grade class! Also, there was Kevin, Tim's brother who lived in Shanghai. The mystery man turned out to be Gary, Tim's brother from New York. We posed for a photo. I was seated in a place of honor on "Grandpa's" left, and on his right were "Grandma" and Kevin. Later, Tim gave me a large framed copy of that family photo.

The Guo family had a good relationship with faculty and staff. Annually, they engaged a restaurant for a Qingdao International School banquet. All of us in QIS regardless of position at school were invited to an evening of feast and fun. In addition to this celebration, Tim ensured that teachers and staff were invited to many city functions and events.

Traditional Chinese wedding and celebrations are held in hotels. I had been to eight of them but the ninth one – the marriage of John, a university professor in Taipei, Taiwan and Amanda – was special because I was the speaker. How she chose me, I had no idea. What the qualification was for a speaker, I did not know. But one thing I know was that we were good friends.

In the Chinese way, Amanda invited me to speak, but not until the night before the wedding.

"Mrs. Munn, could you speak at my wedding tomorrow?"

"Oh? Of course! What do you want me to talk about?" I replied.

"Oh, please speak on love and marriage. There will be an interpreter," she said.

I looked at the clock and it was 9:30; tomorrow at 11:00 would be the wedding. What in the world would I talk about? Then I visualized the audience – a mixed group of young and old. I decided to compare marriage to making sandwich and to cooking soup.

The interpreter turned out to be a local TV news anchor – very tall, handsome and having a good command of English. He read my speech and laughed, looked at me and said, "I never heard of comparing marriage to making sandwiches or soup."

"You have now," I replied.

He continued laughing, and to me, it was a good sign that the audience would be receptive. He and I had so much fun and the bride and groom smiled, listening to this speech:

LOVE AND MARRIAGE

"Today we celebrate the marriage of Amanda and John (Jiang Yan). Love is the foundation of a good marriage. But love is not enough. Success in marriage does not happen overnight. It is a not a quick fix: married today and tomorrow it is successful.

NO. Marriage is not like making a sandwich. Put a slice of tomato and lettuce and mayonnaise to make it taste better between two pieces of bread. NO. To make a marriage succeed is like making Chinese soup. It requires choosing right vegetables, spices, and meat.

LOVE is the water you put in a pot. But water alone does not make soup. You have to add ingredients – vegetables, meat, and spices. Chopping vegetables, preparing spices, and cutting meat take time and patience. Is the knife sharp? If not, you sharpen the knife. Cooking the soup requires that coals are burning, and if it is an electric stove, the temperature must be just right. You feed more coals or adjust stove temperature. Cooking the soup takes time. You have to taste it. Does it need more salt?

Likewise it is in marriage. LOVE is the basic foundation but love alone is not enough. It takes time to nurture a relationship between husband and wife. It requires patience, understanding, respect, listening to each other, feeding your mind with good thoughts of each other, forgiving, solving problems together. Those are the "vegetables." For "meat and spices" to savor a flavorful marriage, you need faith, perseverance and enduring love for each other.

Finally, 'Love is patient and kind, never jealous, never boastful or proud, never haughty, or selfish or rude. It does not demand its own way. It is not irritable or touchy.' (I Corinthians 13: 4-5) You will be loyal to each other no matter what the cost.

Congratulations and may God bless you and your marriage."

RETURNING HOME TO THE USA

"Home is where you are," as Mert once said. Although I maintained residences in the Philippines and in the United States, Qingdao had been my home for four years. By the spring of 2005 I had accomplished 80% of my mission for the Philippines and personal affairs in the United States were requiring my attention. So, I had to come home and I told the QIS Principal that I would not be returning for the next school year.

Thus, my life with ease and joyous teaching in Qingdao International School ended in that spring. I knew that I would miss the relationships that I had cultivated with students, parents, and numerous Chinese friends. I was grateful to the owners, the administrators and faculty and staff of Qingdao International School.

I decided to return to Balabagan before going home to the USA. Ben met me in Manila and escorted me to Davao City and on to Balabagan. While at Shalom Learning School, I had conferences with teachers and gave a workshop on "Integration of Math, Science, and English." I sat in classrooms and observed "problem" children, who were reported to me and worked out solutions.

Courtesy of a generous donor, I also arranged for teachers and staff to go on an education tour to Silliman University. Then, Ben and I took our siblings on a "Seniors Tour" to five provinces in Mindanao to visit schools where we had attended. Jovencia Hofer was very happy to set foot on the grounds of her old school – Bukidnon Normal School in Malaybalay --where before World War II she was in teacher-training. Now it is Bukidnon State University. This trip gave everyone a chance to see places they had not seen in a long time and they were grateful. I felt immense pleasure in giving them this chance to travel.

I had a productive work vacation and an enjoyable visit with family. I realized that I had finally come to grips with being a widow, and my China experience completely healed me. I flew back to the USA wondering what would come next. "The Lord is my Pilot and the Bible is my Compass."

CHAPTER 19

"Glory be to God.....who is able to do far more
than we would ever dare to ask or even dream of
– infinitely beyond our highest prayers, desires, thoughts, or hopes."
(Ephesians 3:20 TLB)

THE DESERT WILL BLOOM AGAIN

Home again in the USA! I arrived in Eugene, Oregon on July 7, 2005 from China. Gideon and Rachel and our dear friends, Bill and Myrna Sweet met me. We would rendezvous whenever I arrived from overseas and visit over dinner.

I went with Gideon and Rachel to Corvallis to rest and to pick up my van. A friend and I drove to Seattle to attend the Quality Schools International (QSI) dinner for its 150 new teachers. I was not one of them but I did express an interest in substituting in any of its schools anywhere in the world. At the dinner, the Vice President offered me a teaching position in one of their schools in Russia. A few days later, when I had lunch in Spokane with the QSI President and his wife, he mentioned four more countries where I could teach. I was tempted to go to Belarus but . . . I was not really available.

I had been away from Spokane and Medical Lake for four years and this time, I was confronted with home repairs, grounds upkeep, physical examinations and personal affairs. It took the remainder of that summer of 2005 and throughout fall to do all the things that required my attention. Those few months were a slack tide in my journey. I did not foresee a new and interesting surge coming.

In late October, after having dealt with the backlog of home maintenance, I received an email from Dr. Larae Palmanter, the same lady who hired me five years before to teach in China. She was now the director of the International Program (IP) of Colegio San Lorenzo in Copiapo, Chile. She let me know of a teaching job at the school. I replied that I was interested and within a few weeks, I was hired and invited to visit the school before it closed that December. (The school year in Chile runs from February to December, which is the beginning of summer in the Southern Hemisphere.)

I flew to Santiago, Chile and to Copiapo up north in the Atacama Desert (Desierto de Atacama). I met the students, parents and school officials. The company would give me free housing and we had to find a rental house while I was there. We found a gated stucco house with four bedrooms, a maid's room off the kitchen with a shower, with a carport protected by a sliding door and with a high fence with bougainvilleas reaching over it, hibiscus, poinsettia and other tropical plants. There were a few orange and lemon trees in the backyard. Larae also said that the company would provide a gardener and a maid.

I was extremely conscious of the expense it required to have me down there for only ten days. I found out soon enough that my employer was Phelps Dodge International Copper Corporation based in Phoenix, Arizona. It has mines in Chile and Colegio San Lorenzo was a school for children of all mine employees, including a few North Americans. It was a fairly large school from kindergarten to high school.

What a trip! I came home to pack my personal belongings that winter to ship to Copiapo, Chile. It would become my home for two years. South America had not been on my list but then again, God's plan for my life was bigger and better. I filled the spot where I was needed. A new beginning on another continent!

COPIAPO, CHILE IN THE ATACAMA DESERT (Desierto de Atacama)

On February 6, 2006, I flew to Dallas/Fort Worth in Texas, where I took an American Airlines flight to Santiago and then Lan Chile Airline to Copiapo. Larae met me at the Desierto de Atacama airport. It was almost the beginning of fall season in the Southern Hemisphere. A thick fog blanketed the whole desert. Specks of green from trees peered through the thick fog. I was surprised to see vineyards and wondered how they could get water when there was no rain at all. Atacama Desert is one of the driest, if not the driest desert in the world.

I found out soon enough that fog catcher supplied the water that made plants grow. Fog catcher is made of special plastic netting strung on posts across the field to catch fog. As fog passes through the net, water vapor is trapped and turns into droplets, which roll down into pipes that are connected to water collection tanks. One fog catcher collects liters and liters of water a day for agriculture. While the valley residents in Copiapo use this water system also for drinking, the city itself sits on an aquifer with water from the Andes Mountains.

Nestled in a valley between bare mountains, Copiapo is a city of about 200,000 and is about 70 kilometers away from the Pacific Ocean. Located in the Atacama Desert, it is the capital of Region 3 in North Chile. I liked driving on Ruta Panamericano (The Pan-American Highway) to Bahia Englesa (English Bay) with friends or to Vallener, a two-hour drive south where there is a Middle Eastern restaurant that served the best hamburger with large-cut fries and baklava. The owners – a man from the Middle

East and his Chilean wife had met in the United States when they were students and decided to relocate in Chile. Vallenar is right on the edge of the desert area called "Desierto Florido," (Flowering Desert).

The vast desert at the foot of bare mountains from Vallenar to Copiapo would burst into a glorious splendor with desert flowers whenever it rained, which is "once in a blue moon."

The landscape remains brown and seeds are dormant for a few years and as soon as rain comes, the desert would bloom again. It bloomed the year before I arrived in Chile, and a few years after I left. I only saw pictures but I often drove through Vallenar -- the perfect stop for a hamburger lunch on our way south to La Serena. Larae and I had been down there on a tour of Elqui Valley in the Andes Mountains. I also took my niece, Bing from Australia and friends Nancy and Judy from Medical Lake on tour of Elqui Valley.

"CASA DOS" (House #2) – the house where I lived -- was three miles from the Colegio San Lorenzo. The trees along the streets looked very dusty because there was no rain at all. The master bedroom had a sliding door that opened to the yard. The fourth bedroom was converted into an office and I used its cabinets for my rock and shell collections. There was no central heating but two portable gas heaters heated the hallway and living room. The dining room and kitchen were equipped with sets of glasses, dishes and silverware for twelve people. The maid came daily to clean and wash dishes. I was all set for entertaining, until I found out the caste system: I could only invite teachers, like me, a "profesora." It was interesting but discomforting. I had heard of the system, but experiencing it first hand was new to me. I decided to tread cautiously on cultural tradition.

I had to get used to a good many things. The gardener came once a week and I watered the plants and lawn in between. Watering was done by flooding with a hose, not sprinkling. Early on I wondered why there were no sprinklers in stores. The gardener explained to me that water from sprinklers would just dry up quickly in the scorching sun.

COLEGIO SAN LORENZO

Our classrooms on the campus of Colegio San Lorenzo looked out onto an avenue of bananas. Beyond the classrooms was a very large open area on the grounds designated for earthquake evacuation. I had to learn earthquake drills and during earthquakes, which there were many, my responsibility on the field was to check children on my list.

Our North American students were immersed in the Chilean school system, but we had them in the International Program most of the day for our U.S. curriculum subjects. I taught math, language arts, social studies and reading to four students – one in kindergarten, one in second, and two in fifth. Although I missed the classroom dynamics with many students as I had in China, planning for these fast learners was equally a challenge. We used the Harcourt Brace reading series and I planned lessons for a one-on-one instruction with students. They went to physical education with Chilean students but they had art and computer classes in the International Program. In addition to being the director, Larae taught art and planned very engaging and interesting extra-curricular activities. We went on field trips to excavation areas, to the beach, to the gem mountain to collect rocks with semi-precious stones and once, to Pucon, South Chile, to explore a cave. Some parents would usually go with us.

In addition to free housing and utilities, I was also provided with a vehicle. Dodge Dakota was really too big for me, but it was the smallest truck in Phelps Dodge' fleet. Vehicles were parked backwards for easy driving off in case of earthquakes. Parking backwards was my biggest problem! The school parking was tight. I had to arrive very early to have enough space to maneuver. One morning, my parking spot had already been taken, I became distracted, misjudged a post and wham! I rammed the passenger side against it! I had to go to the police to make a report. The company found out that I drive only automatic shift, so a smaller vehicle was ordered. When it came, it was brand new Land Rover Freelander! Later, Paola, my first Spanish teacher (the company gave us free lessons) told me that it was only the second of its kind in the city. I asked, "Why?" "It is too expensive," she said. Oops! No wonder that people looked at me when I drove on city streets. On Sundays I went to Iglesia Presbyteriana de Chile, so I parked behind the Catholic Bishop's vehicle on the street across from the Catholic Church. I knew it was safe there and I walked the six blocks to church.

I attended an old church founded in the early 1800's. The people were friendly and it was nice to see all ages in the congregation. I sang right along with them in Spanish, of course, but I had two bibles – English and Spanish. Pastor Cleto Nunez, from Brazil, invited me to its monthly church breakfast ("desayuno"), where I got to meet many church members.

One Sunday afternoon before I found this church, I went with a friend to the Iglesia Methodista de Chile. Older members of the congregation requested old hymns, so with her keyboard, my friend accompanied the pastor while rehearsing old hymns. I sat there and listened, soon, the pastor asked me to sing with him. Why not? I did and I loved the two hymns – "Senior, mi Dios" (How Great Thou Art) and "Alma, Bendice al Senior" (Praise the Lord). I not only practiced with the pastor but I also sang at the Sunday evening worship service. It ended at 9:00 PM, too late for me on a Sunday night. Although I enjoyed singing, I did not go back. Later, I found Iglesia Presbyteriana de Chile with the help of Darinka, my second Spanish teacher.

To practice my Spanish, I met and talked to people in churches, in shops and in the market. I did my own marketing and cooking. I liked going to open markets for vegetables, fruits and fish and stopping at the supermarkets for excellent bread and pastries. In Chile I was mistaken for a Chilean, so people would say, "buen dia" (buenos dias) – "good morning." Eventually, I learned their Chilean Spanish. However, in Buenos Aires, Argentina, it was Castellan – the same Spanish that I learned in college and from my Grandfather who spoke it fluently.

I traveled in Chile and in Argentina, courtesy of the company which provided us with a generous travel allowance. Larae and I would spend weekends in Buenos Aires - touring, shopping, and taking in a "Tango Dinner Show" at the Carlos Gardel showplace. A dinner of Patagonian salmon and black rice was my favorite. We spent a short vacation in Iquique, an open port city near the Peru border. I took Nancy, Judy and Bing on sightseeing trips to Buenos Aires, Santiago and La Serena on Chile's coast. In Elqui Valley in the Andes Mountains, we toured through vineyards, wineries, papaya and cochineal cactus plantations. (Cochineal is a scale insect which grows in clusters on leaves of large pear cactus. When scraped, the insects turn bloody red or purple and are processed into dye. It is used for red coloring of food, fabric and lipstick.) We went as far as the birthplace of Gabriela Mistral, a Nobel Prize poet and Chilean diplomat.

EASTER ISLAND (Isla de Pascua, Rapa Nui)

I discovered during my last quarter that I had more money in my travel account. So I decided to visit Easter Island. Midway between Chile and Tahiti in the South Pacific, it is the most isolated inhabited place on earth with a population mix of Polynesians and Chileans. It is 27 degrees south of the Equator with a land surface of 180 square kilometers (70 square miles). Its airport, Aeropuerto Matavari, is the most remote airport in the world. Once designated as an "Abort Site for US Space Shuttle," it has become a major commercial lane between South America and the South Pacific. Easter Island is 3,700 kilometers from Santiago, mainland Chile.

Easter Island is at the same latitude as Copiapo where I lived but it is so far away. I had to fly to Santiago to catch my flight. The lingering twilight had given way to darkness when Lan Chile Airlines Boeing 767 landed on Mataveri International Airport on Easter Island. A shimmering moonlight river on the ocean, a salty, gentle breeze, and fragrance of tropical flowers carried me back to my homeland. The island has three names: Rapa Nui – Polynesian; Isla de Pascua – Chilean and Easter Island.

I had long been fascinated by the Moia statues so I took the island tours. That became a problem. We had to write our name and age on the manifest. When I looked at it, I told Marcela, our guide, that I would be the last one to sign. I did not want others to see how old I was. I had seen that the ages on the manifest were 20's, 30's, mostly from Australia and New Zealand. There was one 51-year old from Santiago.

I said to him, "Why are you on this tour -- you're from Chile?"

"I want to improve my English," he replied.

I smiled and nodded. He had lived a few years in the United States when he was a child. His parents were students at a university.

When I looked up at the volcano Rano Raraku and the Moia quarry, and saw that people up there seemed so small, like ants, crawling along the side of the mountain. I asked Marcela, "Are we going up there?"

"Yes," she replied. "How is your heart?"

"Oh, my heart is good, but my legs are short."The uneven trail proved rugged with loose dirt, dried tree limbs, roots, rocks, crags. Resting on a flat rock midway up, I told her that I would just sit there and wait.

She said, "Oh no, we're going down another trail."

Just then a voice said, "Don't worry, I will help you."

The security of the young man's arm made negotiating the steps a breeze! Soon we were looking at the huge statues. It was well worth the climb to the quarry to touch the cold nose of an unfinished giant Moia statue – a rock chisel still on his nostril. His body and extremities had laid supine along the side of the mountain for hundreds of years and will be there for eternity.

Midway downhill, there were a number of carved Moi statues which obviously had not reached the shore.

The climb had been wonderful, but it almost did me in. A most excruciating leg pain woke me up in the night and I realized there I was, alone, in the middle of nowhere in the South Pacific, hurting! I rested in my Hotel Taha Tai cottage until late afternoon. I was hungry, so I hobbled to the dining area near the waterfront. Tropical plants, profuse blooms of bougainvilleas and a view of the ocean took my mind off the pain. I propped up my legs on a chair, drank coffee, and snacked on slices of boiled camote (sweet potato). I waited to see the sunset. The sun was pale, descending slowly through mist towards its destination, when suddenly, out of nowhere, a rainbow appeared! With brilliant colors, the rainbow hugged the width of Easter Island. What an incredible sight!

The following day, I walked the short distance to town but I had to run into a coffee shop -- just in time before a cloudburst poured buckets of water. I sipped cappuccino in an open, roofed veranda. Right in front was a papaya tree with ripe yellow fruit! On the island are acres of guavas - a small pink variety. Horses feed on them and the restaurants serve refreshing guava juice. That evening I went to the Polynesian entertainment and that capped a very memorable six-day vacation on Easter Island.

I went home to Copiapo and enjoyed my last springtime in a place I never would have imagined I would live and teach. Two of my students – brother and sister - were returning to the USA. The third one told me that she might also be returning. We all had to move on.

Two years had passed and my contract ended December 5, 2007. I asked Phelps Dodge office if they could give me a return ticket to the USA by way of the Philippines. Now, that is a round-about way but they approved it! In fact, they gave me a business class ticket. I was so surprised. I wrote back that I would be happy to travel economy. So they compromised – sending me to the Philippines by economy class and returning me to the USA from there by business class.

I left Copiapo remembering my Spanish teacher, Darinka's words, "Es tan facil ser feliz," (It is easy to be happy.) I was sad to leave, but I was happy to remember all the good experiences I had for two years. I am so grateful to Larae, Phelps Dodge officials, my students, parents and the Chileans in Colegio San Lorenzo. I remember the parties in the American compound with parents, students and people in the community. I was very grateful to the company president, who gave a generous donation to Shalom Learning School.

RETURN TO MY ROOTS

On November 30, 2007, I left Copiapo for the last time and I flew to Santiago, Dallas/FW, Narita Airport, Manila, and Davao City – 59 hours "on the road!" Ben met me in Manila and our siblings waited for us in Davao as I had requested. I traveled back to Balabagan with them to work in Shalom Learning School. While in Chile, I funded two short-term mortgage investments on coconut and cassava farms to generate income for the school.

In Balabagan, I celebrated my birthday with a dedication service in the UCCP Church and lunch for the congregation. Then, Ben and I took our siblings and escorts on a "Tobias Roots Tour." The trip included a visit to the Dr. Jose Rizal Shrine in Dapitan,

Zamboanga del Norte, to Dumaguete City, and to Cebu - Ginatilan and Badian - our grandparents' hometowns and Cebu City. My grandparents immigrated to Mindanao in the 1920's.

In Badian, we stayed in Matutinao Beach Resort owned by my relatives. I decided to take my siblings to Badian to enjoy the scenery and to feel the mist while riding a bamboo raft in Kawasan Falls, a legacy of our grandfather, Tatay Julio Duque Tobias. He was assigned the area of Kawasan Falls when the Duque property was divided, but he did not like it because he was a fisherman. He was so disappointed that he did not get the property near the shore, so he immigrated to Mindanao; never mentioned his Cebu heritage to anyone in the family. We found out after he died. My siblings on this tour felt the thrill of it all, as I always did whenever I viewed the falls.

Chile's distance from the Philippines allowed me only two trips to Balabagan during those two years but each time - work at school and time with my family - were most enjoyable. Now, I had to return to the USA and see what would be next.

CHAPTER 20

"They that wait upon the Lord shall renew their strength.
They shall mount up with wings like eagles;
they shall run and not be weary;
they shall walk and not faint."
(Isaiah 40:31TLB)

SUNSET OVER SILVER LAKE

"Es tan facil ser feliz." Watching the sunset over Silver Lake definitely gives me joy. I arrived home in the spring of 2008 after an eight-year absence to work and travel on four continents – Asia, North America, Australia and South America. Teaching stints in China and Chile had generated funds to help build and develop Shalom Science Institute.

Sitting on the porch to watch the sun disappear behind the horizons is a step back in time when Mert and I would silently take in the beauty of it all as darkness stealthily moved in. My greatest enemy after he died was dusk and even now, in lesser frequency, the lingering twilight awakens my emotion until it finally gives way to darkness. It was during one of those times that I decided to get out from the quagmire of self-pity and loneliness. Perplexed but undaunted, I took stock of what I had and searched for my life's purpose, mindful of my personal conviction that "Where He wants me to go, I will go and what He wants me to do, I will do."

It had been a long journey up to this point in time. I reflected on my parents and other departed loved ones who paved the way for me to make a difference in the lives of others. I remember Mama's stroke in 1969. My last recollection of her was at Silliman University Medical Center in Dumaguete in the summer of 1971. She passed on in February, 1973. Papa eventually returned to Balabagan, where he lived an active life with church members and in the company of friends who were homesteaders, like him. Decades later after he left Lanao del Sur to take his family to Davao - a province with a Christian population - he had reconciled himself with living among Muslims in Balabagan, and with fortitude and peace in his heart lived harmoniously among them. He died there in 1984.

I came out of retirement to build bridges. A widow of five years in 2000, I took the first step in my journey of thousands of miles. I left behind a retirement of peace and luxury in my lakeside home with a magnificent view of Silver Lake and went home to rural Philippines. I accepted the challenge to help build and develop a Christian school in my hometown with a population of 60% Christians and 40% Filipino Muslims, right on the heels of "War on Muslim Rebels"

In the heart of ARMM (Autonomous Region of Muslim Mindanao), Balabagan is a remote and impoverished municipality, 600 miles south of Manila in Lanao del Sur, on the island of Mindanao. It has been perceived as a dangerous area and my search for outside organizations to partner with us has not been successful. People ask why I go through all this work in retirement years and my response is, "If not me, who? If not now, when?"

There is a dire need for quality education in Balabagan and the development of a preschool into high school is indeed a fruit of labor of so many who share my vision. In June 2010, we added a high school and Shalom Science Institute will have its first high school graduation in March 2014.   In my quest for a life with purpose in retirement, I found immense joy and satisfaction in what I have done during the last decade to provide an opportunity for children to break the cycle of poverty through education right in their community.

What should I do next? Well, from my home, I have continued my role as education and development consultant for the school. My work for the Munn Foundation, whose main beneficiary is Shalom Science Institute, has kept me busy. We are now preparing to comply with Philippine Government Department of Education (DepEd) mandate to provide education from kindergarten to fourth year high school. Known as "Kindergarten Plus 12," this means adding grades 7 and 8. This also means increasing personnel and constructing more classrooms.

BRIDGING THE GAP: WHERE DOES IT ALL BEGIN?

There is more work to be done to continue building the bridge between Christians and Filipino Muslims, who live with Christians from all over, including those who came to Lanao del Sur in the 1920's as immigrants and acquired homesteads.

Where does it all begin? Building the bridge begins with children, whose formative years are of utmost importance to equip them to be the best that they can be in their adult lives. How? Through interaction of all children daily in school – they study and learn together, they play together, and they also pray together;   through parents –Christians and Muslims –who are crossing cultural and religious barriers; and through development

180

of respect, trust, and acceptance of differences in children and adults.

During this School Year 2013-2014, out of 228 enrolled in elementary and high school, 60% are Muslim, including the Mayor's grandchildren.

Shalom Science Institute will have its first high school commencement on April 4, 2014 with ten young people who are poised to seek opportunities for higher education.

Good relationships have been cultivated. We have seen evidence of these throughout   Shalom's eighteen years existence. Our first Grade Six graduates of 34 children in Year 2004 are adults now, living successfully in communities with their different professions. When a high school building was constructed, the Muslim mayors of Balabagan and Kapatagan donated truckloads of gravel, sand, and fill dirt. Last April 2013 the Lanao District Conference (LDC) of the United Church of Christ held its conference at the Shalom campus.   When the mayor of Balabagan, a Muslim, heard that there were 89 people attending the conference for a week, he donated a cow to be butchered. In addition, he sent his Vice-Mayor, also a Muslim, to welcome the delegates at a meeting at the United Church of Christ in Balabagan.

Where does Shalom go from here? It will continue to build the bridge one brick at a time and span the gap between Christians and Filipino Muslims in my hometown. And where will I be? I will be right in the middle, bridging the gap.

Shalom Science Institute has become a major bridge to promote understanding, peace, and harmony in Balabagan, Lanao del Sur. It is bridging the gap between Christians and Filipino Muslims.

"The Lord is my Pilot and the Bible is my Compass"

Eufemia (Femme) Tobias Munn (Big Sis)

Made in the USA
Charleston, SC
17 May 2014